More of 100

facts you don't know

History, curiosity, records and secrets in the

magic world of Football

Declan R. Kensington

2

Summary

INTRODUCTION

Welcome to the fascinating world of football! The most popular and beloved sport on the planet, bringing together millions of people of all ages, cultures, and nationalities. But what makes football so irresistible and universal? Why does it capture the attention of passionate fans in every corner of the globe? In this introduction, we will explore the reason behind the extraordinary popularity of this sport and I will present to you my book, "More of 100 football facts you don't know".

Football has the power to transcend language, culture, and social barriers. It is a sport that is simple at its core, with the objective of putting the ball into the opponent's net.

This simplicity, combined with its competitive and engaging nature, allows anyone, anywhere, to participate and be enthralled.

Whether it's a child in a remote village or a fervent supporter in the heart of a metropolis, football has the gift of bringing people together in a spirit of belonging and shared passion.

But what makes football so captivating? Is it the suspense of a shot on goal, the thrill of a goal, the technical skills of the players, or the exhilarating energy of the fans? It is all of this and much more.

Football is a theater of emotions, a form of artistic expression where talented players create spectacle with the movement of the ball and their extraordinary abilities. It is a vehicle for values such as discipline, teamwork, loyalty, and determination. And it is precisely this passion for football that has inspired me to share with you "More of 100 football facts you don't know".

This book aims to surprise, inform, and entertain, taking you behind the scenes of this marvelous sport. I have carefully selected more of 100 interesting facts that may not be known to everyone, even to the most ardent fans.

Through these pages, I will take you on a journey through time, exploring the history, iconic players, epic competitions, and astonishing records that have made football what it is today.

Whether you are new fans seeking knowledge or seasoned football enthusiasts looking for further curiosities, this book provides a unique opportunity to delve into the fascinating universe of football.

I hope this reading inspires you to discover more about your favorite sport and to share your passion with others.

Get ready to embark on a journey of learning and fun, where you will uncover extraordinary facts that will make you reflect, marvel, and appreciate the magical world of football even more.

Happy reading, and may the passion for football accompany you on every page!

Chapter 1: Historical Curiosities of Football

1.1   *Football of Ancient Romans: The Game of "Harpastum"*

In ancient Rome, among the numerous entertainment and sports activities practiced, there was a game called "Harpastum." This game, similar to modern football, was loved and played by Romans of all social classes, from soldiers to nobles.

Harpastum was played on a rectangular field, with two teams composed of a variable number of players. The main objective was to maintain control of a spherical ball, made of leather or fabric, and carry it into the opponent's half of the field. The rules of the game were simple, but the intensity and energy exerted by the players were remarkable.

What made Harpastum particularly interesting was the combined use of physical skills, strategy, and strength.

Players had to demonstrate agility in dribbling and passing the ball, as well as significant physical endurance to withstand physical contact with opponents.

It was a tough and competitive game, requiring a good deal of courage and determination.

Harpastum was considered a physical training activity for Roman soldiers.

In fact, training in this game was an integral part of military formation, as it was believed to develop the strength, agility, and teamwork of soldiers. However, the game also spread beyond the military sphere, becoming a beloved form of entertainment for many.

Historical descriptions of Harpastum suggest that it was a fast and dynamic game, with quick and daring actions.

Ancient Roman writers such as Galen and Suetonius mention Harpastum in their writings, depicting it as an exciting and engaging game.

Despite the popularity and importance of Harpastum in ancient Rome, the game gradually declined along with the Roman Empire. The arrival of new cultural influences and the evolution of sports interests led to the disappearance of Harpastum over the centuries.

1.2 *Football Among the Maya: The Mesoamerican Ballgame*

Among the ancient Mesoamerican civilizations, the Maya stood out for their passion for a game called "The Ball Game."

This game, often associated with football, played a significant role in Maya culture, involving religious, social, and even political aspects.

The Mesoamerican ballgame was played on specially constructed courts, characterized by two parallel vertical walls serving as the sides of the field. The main objective of the game was to pass a heavy ball, made of natural rubber or latex, through a stone ring positioned on one of the walls.

However, it was not as simple as it seemed. Players were only allowed to touch the ball with their hips, elbows, or knees, and they had to do everything possible to prevent the ball from touching the ground. The Mesoamerican ballgame was not just a sport but also had profound symbolic significance. The Maya believed that the game represented a cosmic struggle between deities, embodying the battle between day and night, life and death.

It was a sacred ritual involving religious and ceremonial elements, often accompanied by offerings and sacrifices to the gods.

Participating in the ballgame was considered a great honor and a test of skill and courage

Players were trained from a young age and dedicated much of their time to perfecting their physical and technical abilities.

The game was so important that tournaments were sometimes organized between different Maya city-states, serving as a means to resolve disputes or establish alliances.

The culture of the Mesoamerican ballgame was so deeply rooted in Maya society that it was reflected even in art and architecture. Numerous reliefs and bas-reliefs depict scenes of the game, bearing witness to its cultural significance.

Some Maya archaeological sites, such as Chichen Itza, even feature ball courts with their unique characteristics.

1.3 *The mystery of the true birthplace of modern football*

Modern football has become one of the most popular and widely followed sports in the world, but its true birthplace is still a subject of debate and mystery. While football has ancient roots that trace back to various civilizations and cultures, it was in the mid-19th century that the rules and structure of the modern game began to take shape.

The traditional narrative attributes the birth of modern football to the United Kingdom, particularly England. According to this account, the first rules of the game were established by the English Football Association (FA) in 1863, marking the official beginning of organized football. Furthermore, England hosted the first international football tournament, the FIFA World Cup in 1966, cementing its reputation as the home of football.

However, recent historical discoveries and research have shed new light on the origins of modern football. Some scholars argue that the game may have originated in other parts of the world, such as China, Latin America, or Africa, before spreading to Europe.

In 2004, an ancient Chinese manuscript dating back to the 3rd century BC, called "Cuju" (literally meaning "kick ball"), was discovered in the Shanxi province.

Cuju was not only a recreational activity but also held cultural and ceremonial significance in ancient China. It was often practiced during festive occasions, military training, and even as a means to promote physical fitness among soldiers. The game served as a form of entertainment for the masses and was also appreciated at the imperial court, further highlighting its importance within Chinese society.

The widespread popularity of Cuju in ancient China is evident from historical accounts, which describe large-scale tournaments and the presence of professional players. These matches attracted huge crowds, and skillful Cuju players were held in high regard for their athletic abilities and mastery on the field.

The manuscript describes a game that closely resembles modern football, with similar rules and objectives. If the antiquity of this manuscript is confirmed, it could provide evidence that modern football had Chinese origins long before its English counterparts.

The mystery surrounding the true birthplace of modern football continues to intrigue scholars, historians, and football enthusiasts. Whether it be in England, China, or elsewhere, the historical and cultural significance of the game remains a testament to its enduring popularity and the passion it evokes across nations and continents.

1.4   *The incredible origin of the term "soccer"*

The origin of the term "soccer" to refer to football may surprise many, as it seems to have roots far from its modern form. While football is commonly associated with England and its nomenclature, the word "soccer" surprisingly has American origins. The word "soccer" derives from the full term "association football," used to distinguish the game from the more traditional form of rugby football. During the 19th century, football began to spread rapidly to various parts of the world, including the United States. However, in America, the term "football" had already been adopted for another sport: what is now known as American football. To avoid confusion and clearly differentiate the two sports, the term "association football" was shortened to "assoccer." This term gained popularity among sports circles and football enthusiasts in the United States in the late 19th and early 20th centuries. Initially, the use of the term "soccer" was predominant in university settings and among the upper classes, who often had strong ties to British culture. It was an informal way of referring to the game, distinguishing it from American football, which was more popular among high school and college athletes.

In the following years, the term "soccer" also spread to common language and was adopted by various organizations and sports leagues. For example, in the 1970s, the North American Soccer League (NASL) was established in the United States, contributing to the consolidation of the use of the term "soccer" for football.

Interestingly, while the term "soccer" was widely used in the United States, in the United Kingdom and other parts of the world, the term "football" was preferred to identify the game. This has led to some irony, as England is considered the birthplace of modern football but adopted a different term from the United States.

In recent years, the term "soccer" has sparked debates and contrasting opinions. Some consider it a foreign or improper term for football, while others simply see it as an alternative and recognizable expression for the game.

Ultimately, the incredible origin of the term "soccer" demonstrates how language and culture have shaped the evolution of football over time. Despite its American origins, the term "soccer" has become part of the international football vocabulary, representing a curious anomaly in sports terminology.

Currently, the distribution of the use of the two terms is approximately:

"Soccer":

- United States: The term "soccer" is widely used in the United States to refer to football. It is the most common and widespread term in sports and everyday language.
- Canada: In Canada, the term "soccer" is also commonly used to refer to football, although the term "football" is recognized and primarily used for Canadian football.
- Australia: In Australia, the term "soccer" is used to distinguish football from other sports such as rugby and Australian rules football, which are more popular.

"Football":

- United Kingdom: In the United Kingdom, as well as in much of Europe and other parts of the world, the predominant term for football is "football." It is the accepted and widely used term among most people and football institutions.
- Europe: In most European countries, such as Spain, Italy, Germany, and France, the term "football" is widely adopted to refer to football.
- South America: In South America, where football is particularly popular, the terms "fútbol" or

"futebol" are primarily used, which correspond to "football" in their respective languages.

- <u>Africa, Asia, and other regions:</u> In various parts of Africa, Asia, and other regions of the world, the term "football" is commonly used to refer to football.

1.5 *The 1st match on TV*

The first televised soccer match was a groundbreaking event that marked the beginning of a new era for both sports and television entertainment. The historic date was September 30, 1937, when the match between Arsenal and Arsenal Reserves was broadcasted from Highbury Stadium in London, United Kingdom.

The broadcast of this pioneering match was made possible through the joint efforts of the British Broadcasting Corporation (BBC) and an experimental television company called Baird Television Ltd. Although television coverage was still in its early stages and limited to a small number of viewers, the revolutionary potential of television as a medium of communication was evident.

The match was broadcasted live only in a small coverage area, primarily in the London region, using a mechanical camera and a low-resolution signal. However, despite the limited technical quality, the event marked the beginning of a new era in sports broadcasting and captured the attention of an audience fascinated by the potential of television.

The television coverage of this first soccer match was a unique experience for the viewers of that time. The cameras were strategically positioned in the stadium to capture the key actions, but the angles and quality of the shots were much different from what we are accustomed to today. Despite the technical limitations, the broadcast still managed to convey the excitement of the game and allowed the audience to experience the feeling of being present on the field.

The match between Arsenal and Arsenal Reserves attracted a considerable number of television viewers, demonstrating the audience's interest in sports broadcasts. Despite the limited number of available televisions and the restricted coverage area, the event represented a milestone in the evolution of sports broadcasting and paved the way for future television coverage of increasingly extensive sports events.

The significance of this first televised soccer match cannot be underestimated. It laid the foundation for the explosion of popularity in televised sports programs and opened doors to a wide range of sports entertainment opportunities for fans worldwide. Today, television coverage of soccer matches has become an essential part of the sports experience and has transformed soccer into a global spectacle that can be followed by millions of people through the small screen.

Chapter 2: Secrets of Successful Coaches

2.1 *"The Coaches' Notebook" by Sir Alex Ferguson*

In the world of football, few coaches can boast such an exceptional and enduring career as Sir Alex Ferguson, the legendary former manager of Manchester United. But there is one aspect of his approach that has captured the attention of many: his famous "Coaches' Notebook."

Sir Alex Ferguson has a reputation for meticulousness and attention to detail that has contributed to his unprecedented success. His Coaches' Notebook has become an integral part of his working method and a key element in shaping the strategy and preparation of his team.

The notebook, which was a sort of personal diary, contained a wide range of information, ideas, notes, and strategies that Sir Alex Ferguson collected and recorded throughout his career. It was his secret to maintaining a sharp mind and an overview of situations and opponents.

But what made Sir Alex Ferguson's Coaches' Notebook so interesting and unique?

Firstly, it encapsulated a vast amount of knowledge, experiences, and observations accumulated over the years. Ferguson took note of everything, from the technical and tactical aspects of the game to information about opponents and team strategies. This allowed him to have a personal archive of information that was easily accessible and consultable at any time.

Furthermore, it was used to monitor the progress of individual players, document their strengths, areas for improvement, and set personal goals. The notebook provided him with a comprehensive overview of the collective strengths and weaknesses of the team, enabling him to make informed decisions regarding team selection, substitutions, and tactical adjustments. This attention to detail and personalized approach to player management were instrumental in cultivating a winning culture at Manchester United.

But what truly made the notebook special was Ferguson's approach to gathering this information. He didn't just take notes on purely technical aspects of the game; he also delved into the emotional nuances, team dynamics, and individual motivations of the players. He was able to capture details that eluded others, identifying strengths and weaknesses of both his team and opponents.

Ferguson's Coaches' Notebook also became a tool for leadership and motivation. He used his observations and the gathered information to personalize his approach with each player, understanding how to motivate them and bring out the best in them. This ability to connect with players and adapt to their individual needs was one of the keys to Ferguson's success as a coach.

Beyond its practical purpose, Sir Alex Ferguson's Coaches' Notebook has become a symbol of his legendary status in the world of football. It has become an object of curiosity and admiration for fans, players, and coaches worldwide. It represents the legacy of a man who dedicated his life to football, encapsulating the essence of his strategic approach and dedication to perfection.

2.2 *"The Ritual of the Tea Cup" by Arsène Wenger*

Among the most influential and respected football coaches of all time is Arsène Wenger, known for his philosophical approach to the game and innovative team management. But there is a ritual that has accompanied his career for many years: the ritual of the tea cup.

For Arsène Wenger, a cup of tea is much more than a simple hot beverage. It has become an essential part of his process of reflection and preparation before matches. Prior to the start of every important game, Wenger would take a break from the hustle and bustle of the dressing room to dedicate himself to a moment of tranquility and focus.

The ritual would begin with Wenger purchasing a cup of tea from a nearby bar or café close to the stadium. Arsène Wenger loved immersing himself in the atmosphere of the place, breathing in the air of the fans and absorbing the energy of the game about to unfold. It was a moment of connection with football and the passion that surrounds this sport.

Once he obtained his preferred cup of tea, Wenger would retreat to a quiet room inside the stadium or a secluded spot away from prying eyes. Here, he would sit down and slowly savor his tea, immersing himself in an atmosphere of serenity and reflection.

During this precious moment, Arsène Wenger would reflect on the upcoming match. He would analyze the opposing team, study tactics, and try to identify weaknesses to exploit. It was a moment of deep introspection and strategic analysis, where he focused on creating the perfect plan to lead his team to victory. But the ritual of the tea cup was not only limited to tactical preparation. It was also a moment for Arsène Wenger to find inner calm and confidence in himself and his team. As he sipped the tea, he would enter a state of mental concentration and visualize success in his mind. It was a way to emotionally charge himself and mentally prepare for the impending battle on the field.

Once he finished his cup of tea, Wenger would rise, ready to face the match with determination and confidence.

The ritual of the tea cup had become a sort of rite of passage for him, a moment of transition from reflection to readiness for action.

2.3 *"The Post-It Note Tactic" by Carlo Ancelotti*

Carlo Ancelotti, a renowned football coach, is known for his tactical prowess and ability to adapt strategies to different challenges on the field. One particular method that has captured the attention of many is his use of post-it notes.

Ancelotti employs post-it notes as a tool to communicate key instructions and information to his team during matches. This unique and creative approach has proven effective in delivering quick and concise messages to players, enabling them to adapt to in-game situations in real-time.

During matches, Ancelotti always keeps a notepad and pen within reach. Prior to kick-off, he takes notes on the starting lineup, tactics to be followed, and key aspects to focus on. These notes are then transferred onto post-it notes, creating a set of instructions and highlights that can be easily consulted and shared with the players.

The simplicity and immediacy of the post-it note tactic have contributed to its effectiveness. The small size of the post-it notes makes them easy to read and place, allowing players to receive clear and quick instructions without interrupting the flow of the game. Ancelotti uses different colors to differentiate various tactical aspects, ensuring rapid understanding by his players.

Furthermore, the use of post-it notes enables Ancelotti to personalize instructions for each player. Each athlete receives a post-it note with specific indications related to their role and responsibilities. This personalized approach ensures players have a clear understanding of what is expected of them, fostering greater team cohesion.

During matches, Ancelotti utilizes post-it notes to indicate tactical changes, player positioning, and exploitable weaknesses. He places the post-it notes on a tactical board or shows them directly to the players on the field. This immediate method of communication enables the team to adapt quickly to game situations and make informed decisions in real-time.

Ancelotti's post-it note tactic has been admired and appreciated not only by his players but also by football enthusiasts and fellow coaches. This innovative approach showcases his ability to simplify complex concepts and effectively transmit information. It also highlights his attention to detail and capacity to adapt to the specific needs of each match.

The post-it note tactic has become a distinctive symbol of Ancelotti's methodology and exemplifies the importance he places on clear communication and flexible tactics. This approach has contributed to

Ancelotti's success as a coach, allowing his team to adapt to challenges and achieve positive results.

2.4 *Why Bielsa is nicknamed "el loco"*

Marcelo Bielsa, also known as "El Loco" for his eccentric lifestyle and unique playing philosophy, is an Argentine football coach with a reputation for originality and peculiarities

One of Bielsa's unusual aspects is his dedication and commitment to tactical analysis. It is said that Bielsa spends hours studying match videos, analyzing opponents' strategies, and identifying weaknesses. He is so obsessed with analysis that he sometimes conducts detailed research on opposing teams, even those in minor leagues or youth squads. This level of dedication and depth in tactical analysis is considered quite unusual in the world of football.

Another peculiar aspect of Bielsa is his eclectic and unconventional attitude. It is said that during his press conferences, Bielsa shares anecdotes and reflections on philosophical, literary, and even political topics. His speech is often enriched with poetic language and a view of football as an art form. This makes his interviews and press conferences unpredictable and stimulating for journalists and fans alike.

Furthermore, Bielsa is known for his absolute respect for ethics and fair play in football. During a match between his Athletic Bilbao and Paris Saint-Germain in 2013, when an opponent was injured and Bilbao's team had stopped playing as a sign of sportsmanship, one of Bielsa's players scored a goal. Instead of taking advantage of the situation, Bielsa instructed his players to let the opponent score a goal to compensate for the fair action. This fair play gesture became a famous episode and highlighted his view of football as an honest and respectful game.

2.5 *Total football (Rinus Michels)*

One of the most famous winning strategies in the history of football was adopted by Rinus Michels, the Dutch coach who revolutionized the game in the 1970s with his approach known as "Total Football" or "Totaalvoetbal."
Michels introduced a new tactical vision that aimed to create a team capable of exerting constant pressure on the opponent and dominating the game in every sector of the field. His strategy was based on:

• Versatility of players: In total football, every player must be able to perform different roles and tasks during the match. This requires comprehensive training and a deep understanding of the responsibilities of each position. Forwards can drop back to support the midfield, while defenders can advance to participate in the offensive action.

• Mobility and fluidity: The team moves in a coordinated and dynamic manner on the field, constantly creating free spaces and passing opportunities. Players must be able to quickly adapt to changes in position and game action, ensuring fluidity and continuity in ball movement.

• Intense pressing: Total football relies on aggressive and coordinated pressing to force the opponent into making mistakes and quickly regain possession of the ball. The team constantly attacks the opponent, putting pressure on opposing players and preventing them from building offensive actions.

• Interchangeability: Players are capable of swapping positions during the match, allowing the team to maintain control of the game and adapt to real-time situations. This creates confusion in the opposing defense and makes it difficult to effectively mark the attackers.

• Involvement of all departments: In total football, there is no strict distinction between defense, midfield, and attack. Every player is involved in the offensive and defensive actions, creating a collective game where all departments work together to achieve objectives.

Michels' total football reached its peak in 1974 when he led the Dutch national team to the World Cup final. Despite their defeat against West Germany, their performance was praised for their technical ability, vision of the game, and innovative approach.
Michels' total football strategy has influenced many subsequent coaches, including Johan Cruyff and Pep

Guardiola. His legacy in football is evidenced by the continued influence of his ideas and the reputation he left behind as one of the great innovators of the game.

Chapter 3: Surprising Facts about World Competitions

3.1 *"The Shortest Match in World Cup History" - Netherlands vs. Costa Rica, 1974*

The shortest match in World Cup history occurred in 1974 during the tournament held in West Germany. It was a clash between the Netherlands and Costa Rica, two teams eager to prove their worth on the world stage.

On June 15, 1974, at the Westfalenstadion in Dortmund, the two teams took to the field for their group stage encounter. From the very beginning, the Netherlands showcased their potential, attacking with determination and seeking to breach the Costa Rican defense. On the other hand, Costa Rica, aware of the strength of their opponents, organized themselves to resist and counter-attack when possible.

However, no one could have anticipated what would unfold in the opening minutes of the game. Just 14 seconds after the kickoff whistle, the Netherlands managed to score a spectacular goal. Johan Neeskens was the one to achieve this incredible feat, after a quick combination of passes between his teammates.

The early goal by the Netherlands shook Costa Rica, who found themselves trailing from the first moments. The Costa Rican team, however, did not surrender easily and tried to react. Nevertheless, the Netherlands maintained control of the game, exerting constant pressure on the opposing defense and seeking to extend their lead.

Despite Costa Rica's attempts to mount a comeback, the Netherlands remained in control of the game and continued to search for more goals. After just eight minutes, they managed to score again, further increasing their advantage and putting additional pressure on Costa Rica.

At that point, the fate seemed sealed. The Netherlands had taken full control of the match and appeared destined for a resounding victory. However, suddenly, something unexpected happened: a violent storm broke out, accompanied by thunder and lightning.

For safety reasons, the referee decided to suspend the match. The players were forced to seek shelter in the dressing rooms as the storm raged on at the stadium. Minutes passed, and the hope of resuming the game dwindled.

After a wait of over an hour, the referee made the final decision to abandon the match due to adverse weather conditions. Although the game was suspended so early, the Netherlands could enjoy the victory and the earned points, solidifying their position in the tournament.

3.2 "The record for the most goals scored by a player in a single tournament" - Just Fontaine, France, 1958

Just Fontaine, a French forward, holds the remarkable record for the most goals scored by a player in a single tournament. This extraordinary feat took place during the 1958 FIFA World Cup held in Sweden.

Fontaine arrived at the tournament with great determination and ambition, aiming to make a significant impact on the world stage. Representing France, he showcased his natural talent and a keen eye for goal throughout the competition.

France faced formidable opponents in a challenging group, but Fontaine remained undeterred. He began his goal-scoring spree from the very first match, displaying remarkable precision and composure in front of the opposition's net.

As the tournament progressed, Fontaine's goal-scoring prowess continued to impress. Match after match, he demonstrated his lethal finishing ability, capitalizing on every opportunity that came his way. Defenders struggled to contain him, and goalkeepers often found themselves helpless against his accurate and powerful strikes.

Fontaine's most memorable performance came in the group stage match against Germany. On that occasion, he netted an astonishing four goals, showcasing his exceptional ability to find space and convert chances. The spectators in the stadium were left in awe as Fontaine etched his name into World Cup history.

The record-breaking moment arrived in the third-place play-off against West Germany. With his goal in that match, Fontaine's tally for the tournament reached a remarkable 13 goals. It was an unprecedented achievement, surpassing any previous goal-scoring record in World Cup history.

Notably, Fontaine achieved this remarkable feat despite France failing to reach the final of the tournament. Despite the disappointment of missing out on the ultimate prize, Fontaine's individual accomplishment earned him immense respect and admiration from fans and opponents alike.

Just Fontaine's legacy in football has endured over the years.

His record of the most goals scored by a player in a single tournament remains unbroken to this day. It stands as a testament to his exceptional goal-scoring ability and unwavering dedication to the game. Fontaine continues to be an icon in the world of football, with his name forever etched in the annals of World Cup records.

3.3 "The 10 fastest goals in the history of the FIFA World Cup"

- <u>Hakan Şükür - Turkey vs. South Korea, 2002 - 11 seconds</u>: Hakan Şükür holds the record for the fastest goal in World Cup history. In the opening match of the 2002 tournament, he found the back of the net just 11 seconds after the kickoff, surprising everyone with his lightning-fast strike.
- <u>Vaclav Masek - Czechoslovakia vs. Mexico, 1962 - 16 seconds</u>: Vaclav Masek scored an early goal in the 1962 World Cup when he found himself in the right place at the right time to put the ball into the net just 16 seconds into the match.
- <u>Ernst Lehner - Germany vs. Austria, 1934 - 25 seconds</u>: In the 1934 World Cup, Ernst Lehner of Germany wasted no time in making an impact. He scored a goal only 25 seconds after the kickoff, setting a record that would stand for many years.
- <u>Bryan Robson - England vs. France, 1982 - 27 seconds</u>: Bryan Robson's goal in the 1982 World Cup came early in the match against France. With just 27 seconds on the clock, Robson capitalized on a defensive error and gave England an early lead.

- <u>Celso Ayala - Paraguay vs. Nigeria, 1998 - 56 seconds</u>: Celso Ayala of Paraguay found the back of the net just 56 seconds into the match against Nigeria in the 1998 World Cup. His quick goal set the tone for an exciting encounter.
- <u>Miroslav Klose - Germany vs. Brazil, 2014 - 68 seconds:</u> Miroslav Klose became the all-time leading scorer in World Cup history during the 2014 tournament. In the semifinal match against Brazil, he scored just 68 seconds into the game, contributing to Germany's historic 7-1 victory.
- <u>Bernard Lacombe - France vs. Italy, 1978 - 90 seconds</u>: Bernard Lacombe scored an early goal for France in their 1978 World Cup encounter against Italy. He took just 90 seconds to find the back of the net, giving his team an early advantage.
- <u>Bobby Charlton - England vs. Mexico, 1966 - 120 seconds</u>: Bobby Charlton, a key player in England's victorious 1966 World Cup campaign, scored a goal just 2 minutes into their group stage match against Mexico.
- <u>Robin van Persie - Spain vs. Netherlands, 2014 - 122 seconds</u>: Robin van Persie's memorable diving header against Spain in the 2014 World Cup caught the attention of football fans

worldwide. He scored the goal only 122 seconds into the match, setting the stage for the Netherlands' 5-1 victory.

- <u>Andrés Guardado during the match between Mexico and the Netherlands in 2014.</u> The goal came after 129 seconds of play, making Guardado one of the players to have scored a goal very quickly in the World Cup competition.

3.4 _The national football teams that have never participated in a World Cup._

These teams represent the continents that have not had the participation of a national team in the FIFA World Cup.

Africa:

- Comoros
- Eritrea
- Mauritania
- São Tomé and Príncipe
- Seychelles
- Swaziland (Eswatini)

North and Central America:

- Anguilla
- Aruba
- Bermuda
- Dominica
- Cayman Islands
- United States Virgin Islands
- Montserrat
- Saint Kitts and Nevis

- Saint Lucia
- Saint Vincent and the Grenadines
- Turks and Caicos Islands

South America:

- French Guiana

Asia:

- Burma (Myanmar)
- Bhutan
- China
- North Korea
- Macau
- Palestine
- Tibet

Europe:

- Andorra
- Gibraltar
- Kosovo
- Liechtenstein
- Monaco
- San Marino

- Sint Maarten
- Vatican City

Oceania:

- Falkland Islands (Malvinas)
- Niue
- Tahiti
- Tokelau
- Tonga
- Tuvalu
- Wallis and Futuna

3.5 *"the hand of God"*

One of the most blatant referee errors in the history of the FIFA World Cup occurred during the 1986 tournament in Mexico. It was known as the "Hand of God" incident involving Diego Maradona in the quarterfinal match between Argentina and England.

On June 22, 1986, during the first half of the game, Maradona scored a goal that would become one of the most iconic moments in football history. However, what made it famous was the way he scored that goal. In the 51st minute, Maradona jumped to reach a cross inside the penalty area. Using his left hand, he punched the ball into the net. The Tunisian referee, Ali Bin Nasser, failed to detect the offense and allowed the goal to stand, despite protests from the English players.

Later, Maradona referred to that goal as the "Hand of God," admitting that he had scored with his hand. Television replays clearly showed the foul play, but the referee did not have access to such technology at the time and could not review the action.

This incident sparked a lot of debate and controversy, as the referee's decision influenced the final outcome of the match. Argentina went on to win 2-1 and eventually won the tournament.

Despite the English protests and the clear violation of the rules, the referee's decision stood, making Maradona's action one of the most evident and discussed referee errors in the history of the FIFA World Cup.

Chapter 4: Epic Football Rivalries

4.1 *The Fiercest Club Rivalries: History of English Rivalries*

England boasts some of the most intense and passionate football rivalries in the world, with derbies that have captivated fans for over a century. These rivalries go beyond mere competition; they are deeply ingrained in the history and identity of the clubs and their respective cities. Let's explore some of the hottest English derbies and understand why each one holds a special place in the hearts of football fans.

A. Manchester United vs. Manchester City - The Manchester Derby:

Known as the Manchester Derby, this rivalry pits two football giants from the same city against each other. Manchester United and Manchester City are both located in the North West of England, but their histories, fan bases, and styles of play differ significantly. The rivalry intensified in recent years due to City's rise in prominence and significant financial investment, challenging United's traditional dominance. Matches between the two clubs are always fiercely contested, with local bragging rights at stake.

B. <u>Liverpool vs. Everton - The Merseyside Derby:</u>

The Merseyside Derby is a clash between Liverpool's two football powerhouses, Liverpool FC and Everton FC. Both clubs share the city of Liverpool, separated only by a park, yet they have developed unique identities and fan bases.

The rivalry dates back to the 19th century and is fueled by the working-class roots of both clubs' supporters.

The Merseyside Derby is known for its raw passion and intense atmosphere, with families often divided between red and blue loyalties.

C. <u>Arsenal vs. Tottenham Hotspur - The North London Derby:</u>

The North London Derby is a clash between two fierce rivals from the capital city, Arsenal and Tottenham Hotspur.

The rivalry goes beyond football, encompassing the contrasting identities of North London neighborhoods.

Arsenal, based in Islington, is associated with a more affluent fan base, while Tottenham, situated in Haringey, draws its support from a more diverse and working-class community. Matches between the two teams are always closely contested and filled with drama, as both clubs vie for supremacy in the city.

D. <u>Newcastle United vs. Sunderland - The Tyne-Wear Derby:</u>

The Tyne-Wear Derby represents the fierce rivalry between Newcastle United and Sunderland, two clubs located in the North East of England.

The rivalry stems from historical economic and industrial differences between the two cities.

Matches between these clubs are often referred to as "High Stakes Clashes" as they carry immense significance for both sets of fans.

Relegation battles and promotion races have added further spice to this already intense rivalry.

E. <u>Aston Villa vs. Birmingham City - The Second City Derby:</u>

Known as the Second City Derby, this rivalry brings together Aston Villa and Birmingham City, two clubs from the city of Birmingham.

The rivalry is born out of the geographical proximity of the clubs and their strong supporter bases.

Matches between the two teams are fiercely contested, with both clubs' fans eagerly awaiting the chance to claim supremacy in the city.

F. <u>West Ham United vs. Millwall - The East London Derby:</u>

The East London Derby involves West Ham United and Millwall, two clubs from the East End of London.
This rivalry is characterized by its fiery nature, with a history of crowd trouble and intense animosity between the fan bases. Matches between West Ham and Millwall are often emotionally charged and high-octane affairs.

4.2 *National Team Rivalries: Battles for Supremacy and Regional Pride*

While club rivalries ignite passions at the domestic level, national team rivalries take football's intensity to a whole new level.

Matches between national teams transcend club loyalties, uniting fans from different walks of life under the banner of their country.

These battles for supremacy and regional pride fuel international football competitions and evoke an unparalleled sense of national identity. Let's explore some of the most iconic national team rivalries and the historical significance that makes them truly special.

A. **England vs. Germany - The Battle of Nations:**

The rivalry between England and Germany is deeply rooted in history, with echoes of World War II adding emotional weight to their encounters. Often referred to as the "Battle of Nations," the rivalry is marked by intense competition and mutual respect.

Matches between these footballing giants have provided some of the most memorable moments in football history, with both nations eager to prove their dominance on the global stage.

B. Brazil vs. Argentina - The Battle of South America:

The rivalry between Brazil and Argentina is one of the most celebrated in international football.

These South American powerhouses have a long-standing rivalry that goes back to the early days of football in the region.

The fierce competition between two footballing juggernauts, often producing skillful displays and dramatic moments, adds to the allure of their matchups.

Matches between Brazil and Argentina are more than just football games; they are clashes between two football-crazy nations vying for regional supremacy.

C. Italy vs. Germany - The European Powerhouses:

Matches between Italy and Germany are characterized by tactical brilliance and hard-fought battles.

These two European footballing giants have a history of intense encounters, especially in major international tournaments.

The rivalry represents a clash of footballing philosophies, with Italy's renowned defensive prowess up against Germany's free-flowing attacking style. The matches between these two powerhouses are a true spectacle for football fans worldwide.

D. <u>Spain vs. Portugal - The Iberian Derby:</u>

The Iberian Derby brings together Spain and Portugal, two neighboring nations with a shared history and cultural ties. The rivalry extends beyond football, reflecting the historical relationship between the two Iberian Peninsula countries.

Their encounters are marked by flair, creativity, and technical brilliance, making them a treat for football purists.

Matches between Spain and Portugal ignite a sense of pride and unity among their respective populations, adding an extra layer of significance to this rivalry.

E. <u>USA vs. Mexico - The CONCACAF Showdown:</u>

In the CONCACAF region, the rivalry between the United States and Mexico is arguably the most significant.

Matches between these two nations are heated affairs, both on and off the pitch, with passionate fan bases adding to the intensity.

The rivalry represents a battle for regional dominance and serves as a litmus test for the progress of football in North America.

Matches between the USA and Mexico have the power to unite their respective nations and bring football to the forefront of public consciousness.

F. Italy - The Historic Showdown:

France and Italy share a long history of intense football battles, making their encounters highly anticipated by fans worldwide.

The rivalry has seen iconic moments, including epic clashes in major tournaments, with both nations producing generations of footballing legends.

Matches between France and Italy are tactical battles of the highest order, with an emphasis on defensive solidity and flair in attack.

G. Netherlands vs. Belgium - The Low Countries Derby:

The rivalry between the Netherlands and Belgium, often referred to as the Low Countries Derby, stems from their geographical proximity and shared history.

Matches between these two neighbors are competitive, with both teams eager to assert their footballing prowess within the region.

The rivalry serves as a celebration of the cultural ties between the two countries, creating an atmosphere of mutual respect and healthy competition.

4.3 *The Origins of Iconic Rivalries: Hatred Born on and off the Pitch*

Iconic football rivalries are not just a product of chance; they often have deep-rooted origins that go beyond the boundaries of the pitch. These intense competitions between clubs or national teams are fueled by historical, cultural, and geographical factors, creating a backdrop of animosity and passion. Let's delve into the origins of some of football's most iconic rivalries and understand the reasons behind the deep-seated hatred between teams and their fans.

A. **Longstanding grudges:**

A prime example of a rivalry born from longstanding grudges is the "Old Firm Derby" between Celtic and Rangers in Scotland.

This intense rivalry is one of the oldest and most fiercely contested derbies in football history.

The roots of the Old Firm Derby trace back to the late 19th century when Celtic and Rangers were established in Glasgow.

The rivalry between the two clubs goes beyond football, with historical religious and societal tensions playing a significant role in fueling the animosity.

Celtic, often associated with the Catholic community in Glasgow, was founded to provide support for Irish immigrants.

On the other hand, Rangers, with a Protestant following, was formed to act as a counterbalance to Celtic and cater to the Protestant community.

The deep-seated religious and cultural differences between the two fan bases have given rise to a heated and at times hostile atmosphere during Old Firm matches.

This rivalry extends beyond the 90 minutes on the pitch and is deeply ingrained in the identities of the clubs and their supporters.

The Old Firm Derby is marked by its passionate atmosphere, with both Celtic Park and Ibrox Stadium filled to capacity with fervent fans.

Matches between Celtic and Rangers are often closely contested, and the desire to claim bragging rights over the other club adds an extra layer of intensity to the encounters.

Unfortunately, the historical tensions between Celtic and Rangers have, at times, spilled over into incidents of sectarian violence and bigotry, making it essential for authorities to maintain strict security measures during these fixtures.

The Old Firm Derby represents more than just a football match; it symbolizes a complex web of historical, cultural, and social factors that have shaped the identities of both clubs and their supporters.

The rivalry between Celtic and Rangers remains a poignant reminder of the power of football to reflect and influence society.

B. Regional Identity and Pride:

Another prime example of a rivalry born from regional identity and pride is the "Derby della Madonnina" between AC Milan and Inter Milan in Italy. This intense rivalry, also known as the Milan Derby, is one of the most significant fixtures in Italian football.

AC Milan and Inter Milan both call the city of Milan home, and their histories are deeply intertwined with the city's rich cultural heritage.

The clubs were founded in the early 20th century, and their supporters come from different areas of the city, each with its distinct characteristics.

AC Milan was historically associated with the more affluent and aristocratic neighborhoods of Milan, while Inter Milan's fan base came from the working-class districts.

This class divide contributed to the initial tensions between the two clubs and fueled the rivalry.

The Derby della Madonnina is characterized by its electric atmosphere and heated contests on the field. Matches between AC Milan and Inter Milan are often fiercely contested, with both teams and their fans desperate to claim bragging rights in the city.

The rivalry extends beyond football, impacting local culture and everyday life in Milan.

The passion and intensity displayed by the players and fans during the Milan Derby have produced countless memorable moments in football history. From iconic goals to dramatic comebacks, the Derby della Madonnina remains a fixture that captivates fans and evokes a sense of pride and unity among Milanese supporters.

Off the pitch, the rivalry between AC Milan and Inter Milan extends to transfer battles and player acquisitions.

The Milan Derby represents more than just a football match; it represents the soul of a city divided by passion for the sport. The colors red and black of AC Milan and blue and black of Inter Milan adorn the city, and the Derby della Madonnina stands as a symbol of Milan's footballing heritage and its people's unwavering loyalty to their respective clubs.

C. Competing for Supremacy:

The rivalry between Real Madrid and FC Barcelona, often referred to as "El Clásico," is one of the most iconic and intense rivalries in the world of football. These two Spanish football giants have a storied history of competition and dominance in both domestic and international competitions. The rivalry is deeply rooted in historical, cultural, and political factors, making it much more than a mere football clash.

The origins of the rivalry between Real Madrid and Barcelona can be traced back to the early 20th century when both clubs were founded.

Real Madrid was established in 1902, while FC Barcelona was founded in 1899.

From the beginning, the two clubs represented different regions and cultural identities within Spain: Catalonia, represented by Barcelona, and Castile, represented by Madrid.

Catalonia, with its distinct language and culture, has a long history of seeking greater autonomy and independence from the central government in Madrid.

The rivalry between Real Madrid and Barcelona, therefore, goes beyond the football pitch and reflects the broader political and cultural tensions within Spain.

The matches between the two clubs are seen as a symbolic battle between the Spanish central government and the aspirations of the Catalan people.

Over the years, Real Madrid and Barcelona have been the most successful clubs in Spanish football, dominating domestic competitions and European tournaments.

This competition for supremacy has further fueled the rivalry.

Both clubs boast a rich history of winning domestic league titles and UEFA Champions League trophies, often surpassing the achievements of other Spanish clubs.

The rivalry has been intensified by the contrasting approaches to player recruitment and development. Real Madrid, known for its "Galácticos" policy, has often splurged on big-name, high-profile players from around the world.

In contrast, Barcelona prides itself on its youth academy, "La Masia," which has produced world-class talents like Lionel Messi, Andres Iniesta, and Xavi Hernandez.

This difference in philosophies adds another layer of competition between the two clubs, with Real Madrid's star-studded lineup facing off against Barcelona's homegrown talents.

One of the most captivating aspects of the rivalry in recent years was the presence of two footballing legends - Lionel Messi at Barcelona and Cristiano Ronaldo at Real Madrid.

Their individual duels and goal-scoring feats added to the intensity of El Clásico.

The battle for supremacy between these two global superstars further elevated the significance of the rivalry on the global stage.

D. **Controversial Encounters and Incidents:**

Certain rivalries are fueled by controversial encounters and incidents that have left a lasting impact on both teams and their supporters. The rivalry between England and Argentina is a prime example. The infamous "Hand of God" incident during the 1986 FIFA World Cup, in which Diego Maradona scored a goal with his hand against England, ignited tensions between the two nations. Subsequent encounters between England and Argentina have been charged with emotion and a desire for revenge.

E. **Historical Significance:**

A rivalry born from historical significance is the "Superclásico" between Boca Juniors and River Plate in Argentina.

This iconic South American derby is one of the most intense and passionate fixtures in football history. Boca Juniors and River Plate are two of the most successful and popular football clubs in Argentina, with a combined total of numerous domestic and international trophies.

The rivalry between these two Buenos Aires-based clubs dates back to the early 20th century, and it is deeply ingrained in Argentine football culture.

The Superclásico is marked by its fierce on-field battles and its impact on Argentine society.

Matches between Boca Juniors and River Plate capture the attention of the entire nation, with streets emptying as fans gather around televisions to watch the spectacle.

The historical significance of the Superclásico is intertwined with Argentine politics and social divisions.

Boca Juniors, with its working-class fan base, is often seen as a representation of the "people," while River Plate, with its middle-class support, is associated with the "elite."

This social divide adds an extra layer of significance to the rivalry.

The Superclásico also transcends football, influencing various aspects of Argentine culture, including music, art, and literature. Tango, an iconic dance genre, emerged in the working-class neighborhoods of Buenos Aires, and its melancholic themes are often associated with the passionate emotions of the Superclásico.

4.4 *Memorable matches that made history*

In the world of football, certain matches go beyond being just games; they transcend the boundaries of sport and become defining moments in the history of iconic rivalries.

These are the matches that are etched into the memories of fans, forever shaping the narratives and intensity of the rivalries.

From dramatic comebacks to historical significance, let's explore some of the most memorable clashes that have defined football rivalries forever.

A. The Miracle of Istanbul - AC Milan vs. Liverpool (UEFA Champions League Final, 2005):

The UEFA Champions League Final in 2005 between AC Milan and Liverpool at the Atatürk Olympic Stadium in Istanbul, Turkey, is widely regarded as one of the most remarkable comebacks in football history. AC Milan, a powerhouse in European football, took an early 3-0 lead in the first half, seemingly cruising to victory.

However, in an astonishing turn of events, Liverpool mounted an epic second-half comeback, scoring three goals in just six minutes.

The match ended 3-3 after extra time, and Liverpool went on to win 3-2 in the penalty shootout.

This victory, against all odds, forever cemented Liverpool's status as a team capable of miracles.

The Miracle of Istanbul showcased the resilience and fighting spirit of Liverpool, and it remains one of the most cherished moments for their fans.

For AC Milan, the defeat was a bitter pill to swallow, and it added fuel to the fire of the rivalry between the two European giants.

B. "La Remontada" - FC Barcelona vs. Paris Saint-Germain (UEFA Champions League Round of 16, 2017):

In the second leg of the UEFA Champions League Round of 16 tie between FC Barcelona and Paris Saint-Germain (PSG), the footballing world witnessed one of the most astonishing comebacks in the history of the competition.

In the first leg, PSG had defeated Barcelona 4-0, putting them in a commanding position for the return fixture.

However, Barcelona staged an incredible comeback at the Camp Nou, winning the second leg 6-1.

This 6-5 aggregate victory, often referred to as "La Remontada" (The Comeback), is etched into the annals of football history and stands as a testament to the spirit and determination of the Barcelona players. "La Remontada" not only solidified Barcelona's reputation as a force to be reckoned with but also dealt a devastating blow to PSG.

The result further intensified the rivalry between the two clubs, leaving a lasting impact on the way fans perceive their encounters.

C. The Aguero Moment - Manchester City Winning the Premier League (2011-2012):

In the 2011-2012 Premier League season, Manchester City and Manchester United engaged in an epic title race that culminated in one of the most dramatic moments in football history.

As the season reached its final day, the two Manchester clubs were separated by just a single point, with Manchester City in pursuit of their first top-flight league title in over four decades.

On May 13, 2012, the final day of the season, Manchester City faced Queens Park Rangers (QPR) at the Etihad Stadium, while Manchester United played Sunderland away.

Manchester City, needing a win to secure the title, found themselves trailing 2-1 deep into stoppage time.

With just seconds remaining, it seemed that the title would slip away from City's grasp.

However, in the 94th minute, the unlikeliest of heroes emerged.

Sergio Aguero, Manchester City's talismanic striker, received a pass inside the QPR penalty box.

With nerves of steel, Aguero steadied himself and fired a thunderous shot into the back of the net, securing a 3-2 victory for Manchester City and clinching the Premier League title.

Aguero's last-gasp goal, often referred to as "Agueroooooo," sparked scenes of jubilation and celebration among the Manchester City players, fans, and coaching staff. It was a moment of pure ecstasy, as decades of frustration and longing for a league title were finally fulfilled.

The Aguero Moment not only marked Manchester City's ascent to the pinnacle of English football but also served as a defining moment in their rivalry with Manchester United.

The two clubs, both based in the city of Manchester, have been fierce competitors for decades, and this thrilling conclusion to the 2011-2012 season further intensified the rivalry.

For Manchester City fans, the memory of Aguero's dramatic goal will forever be etched in their hearts, representing a moment of glory and a turning point in the club's history.

On the other hand, Manchester United fans were left heartbroken, as they witnessed their local rivals snatch the title away in such dramatic fashion.

The Aguero Moment became a symbol of the unpredictability and drama that makes football so enthralling.

It highlighted the fine margins that separate success from failure in the sport and showcased the emotional rollercoaster that fans experience on the journey to glory.

To this day, Aguero's iconic goal remains one of the most unforgettable moments in Premier League history.

The match and its dramatic conclusion have become a significant part of the Manchester City-Manchester United rivalry, adding another chapter to the storied history of football's most enthralling contests.

D. **Watford's Promotion Heroics against Leicester City (Championship Play-Off Semifinal, 2012-2013 Season):**

Watford Football Club's memorable promotion heroics against Leicester City in the Championship Play-Off Semifinal during the 2012-2013 season marked one of the most thrilling and dramatic moments in the club's recent history.

This captivating encounter showcased the heart, determination, and resilience of both teams as they fought for a place in the Premier League.

Throughout the Championship season, Watford had displayed an attacking brand of football under the guidance of manager Gianfranco Zola.

Spearheaded by prolific striker Matej Vydra and the influential Troy Deeney, the Hornets had emerged as one of the standout teams in the division.

In the semifinal, Watford faced Leicester City, a formidable side that had also enjoyed an impressive campaign.

The two-legged tie promised to be fiercely contested, with the winner securing a place in the Championship Play-Off Final at Wembley Stadium.

The first leg took place at Leicester City's King Power Stadium, where the Foxes secured a 1-0 victory, giving them a slender advantage going into the return leg at Watford's Vicarage Road.

In the second leg, played in front of a passionate home crowd, Watford found themselves trailing 2-1 on aggregate until the final minutes of injury time.

With just seconds left on the clock, the Hornets were awarded a corner, and goalkeeper Manuel Almunia joined the attack in a desperate attempt to salvage their promotion dreams.

As the corner was delivered into the box, Almunia rose above the Leicester defense and headed the ball towards the goal. The ball found its way to the feet of Jonathan Hogg, who managed to stab it into the net, sending Vicarage Road into wild celebrations.

The dramatic late equalizer leveled the aggregate score at 2-2 and sent the tie into extra time.

In the additional 30 minutes, both teams fought valiantly, but neither could find a decisive goal.

The tie went to a nail-biting penalty shootout.

In the end, it was Watford's goalkeeper Almunia who emerged as the hero, making two crucial saves to guide the Hornets to a 3-1 shootout victory.

The scenes of jubilation at Vicarage Road were electric, as players, staff, and supporters celebrated together.

The triumphant victory against Leicester City secured Watford's place in the Championship Play-Off Final at Wembley Stadium, where they would face Crystal Palace.

While Watford eventually fell short in the Play-Off Final, the thrilling semifinal victory against Leicester City will always be remembered as a defining moment in the club's journey to reclaim their place in the Premier League.

E. The "Maracanazo" - Brazil vs. Uruguay (FIFA World Cup Final, 1950):

The 1950 FIFA World Cup Final, also known as the "Maracanazo," is one of the most significant matches in football history.

The final, held at the Maracanã Stadium in Rio de Janeiro, Brazil, was contested between Brazil and Uruguay.

With an expectant home crowd, Brazil took the lead early in the second half.

However, Uruguay mounted a remarkable comeback, scoring two goals to secure a 2-1 victory and stun the Brazilian nation.

The result remains one of the biggest upsets in World Cup history and is still seen as a source of deep pain for Brazilian fans.

The "Maracanazo" had a profound impact on football in Brazil, sparking soul-searching and changes in the way the country approached the sport. It also intensified the rivalry between Brazil and Uruguay, becoming a defining moment whenever the two South American nations meet on the football field.

F. The "Battle of Santiago" - Chile vs. Italy (FIFA World Cup Group Stage, 1962):

The group stage match between Chile and Italy in the 1962 FIFA World Cup, known as the "Battle of

Santiago," is remembered for its intense physicality and hostility. The match, held in Chile, saw numerous violent incidents and altercations on the pitch, leading to the sending off of two Italian players and a Chilean player.

The "Battle of Santiago" is notorious for its aggressive and combative nature, with some referring to it as one of the dirtiest matches in football history. The hostility and animosity displayed during the match became a defining moment in the rivalry between Chile and Italy, leaving a lasting impact on the way these two teams approach their encounters.

G. The "Five-Minute Final" - Spain vs. Netherlands (FIFA World Cup Final, 2010):

The final of the 2010 FIFA World Cup, held in South Africa, featured a highly anticipated clash between Spain and the Netherlands. The match was fiercely contested, with both teams vying for their first-ever World Cup title.

The match remained goalless until the 116th minute when Andrés Iniesta scored a dramatic extra-time winner for Spain.

The 1-0 victory secured Spain's first-ever World Cup triumph and marked the culmination of a golden generation of Spanish football.

The "Five-Minute Final" was a moment of triumph for Spain, but it also left a deep sense of disappointment for the Netherlands, who had come so close to claiming their first World Cup. The match became a defining moment in the rivalry between the two nations and intensified the competition whenever they meet on the international stage.

4.5 _Legendary Football Rivalries: Icons of the Beautiful Game_

In the annals of football history, some rivalries have transcended the sport and become cultural phenomena. These iconic duels between footballing legends have captivated fans across generations and continents. They have defined eras, showcased different styles of play, and sparked impassioned debates among supporters. In this chapter, we delve into seven legendary football rivalries, pitting football icons against each other, etching their names forever in the beautiful game's folklore.

A. **Ronaldo vs. Messi: The Battle of Titans**

The rivalry between Cristiano Ronaldo and Lionel Messi is perhaps the most iconic in modern football. For over a decade, these two phenomenal players have dominated the footballing landscape, setting records and winning accolades that seemed beyond human achievement.

Ronaldo, with his imposing physique and explosive athleticism, represents the epitome of power and precision in front of goal.

On the other hand, Messi, with his dribbling wizardry and otherworldly vision, embodies grace and creativity on the pitch.

Their rivalry has played out in both domestic and international competitions, with Ronaldo representing clubs like Manchester United, Real Madrid, and Juventus, while Messi has remained a one-club man at Barcelona.

The debate over who is the better player has raged on for years, dividing fans and pundits alike. However, what is undeniable is that Ronaldo and Messi's rivalry has elevated the sport to new heights and established them as true legends of the beautiful game.

B. <u>Maradona vs. Pelé: The Battle of Legends</u>

Diego Maradona and Pelé are two of the most revered names in football history, each leaving an indelible mark on the sport during their respective eras

Pelé, the Brazilian superstar, won three FIFA World Cups and is often hailed as the greatest footballer of all time. His skill, goalscoring prowess, and sheer dominance on the pitch earned him a legendary status.

Maradona, the Argentine maestro, led his national team to victory in the 1986 FIFA World Cup, single-handedly dismantling opposition defenses with his mesmerizing dribbling and uncanny ability to score crucial goals.

Their rivalry reached its peak during the 1986 World Cup quarterfinal when Argentina faced Brazil. Maradona scored a brilliant goal in that match, forever etching his name in the history books.

While the debate over who is the greatest of all time continues, Pelé and Maradona's rivalry remains a cherished part of football folklore, celebrating two footballing icons who captured the imagination of fans worldwide.

C. Cruyff vs. Beckenbauer: Masterminds of Total Football

Johan Cruyff and Franz Beckenbauer were pioneers of the game, masterminding tactical revolutions that forever changed football.

Cruyff, the Dutch genius, was the embodiment of "Total Football," a philosophy that emphasized fluid attacking play and positional interchangeability. As a player and later as a manager, Cruyff left an indelible mark on the sport, with his influence still felt in modern-day football.

Beckenbauer, the German "Kaiser," was a commanding defender and a visionary leader on the pitch. As a player and coach, he emphasized the importance of organization and strategy, laying the groundwork for the success of German football in subsequent years.

Their rivalry played out during the 1974 FIFA World Cup final, where Beckenbauer's West Germany faced Cruyff's Netherlands.

West Germany emerged victorious, but both Cruyff and Beckenbauer's impact on the sport extended far beyond that match.

Their rivalry exemplifies how football is not just about individual brilliance, but also about tactical innovation and leadership on and off the field.

D. Zidane vs. Ronaldo: The 1998 World Cup Clash

The 1998 FIFA World Cup final saw a memorable duel between two footballing greats, Zinedine Zidane and Ronaldo Nazário.

Zidane, the French maestro, was a midfield magician known for his sublime technique, vision, and ability to deliver in high-pressure situations.

Ronaldo, the Brazilian phenomenon, was a goal-scoring machine with lightning-fast pace and a killer instinct in front of goal.

The final between France and Brazil showcased the clash of these two footballing titans.

Zidane famously scored two headers for France, leading them to a 3-0 victory and their first-ever World Cup triumph.

Despite the disappointment, Ronaldo's rivalry with Zidane remained one of mutual respect.

Both players continued to shine in their respective careers, leaving an enduring legacy in football.

E. Eusebio vs. Pele: The 1966 World Cup Showdown

The 1966 FIFA World Cup witnessed a captivating rivalry between Eusebio da Silva Ferreira, the "Black Panther" from Portugal, and the Brazilian legend, Pelé. Eusebio was Portugal's talisman and an extraordinary goal-scorer, leading his team to a historic third-place finish in the tournament. Pelé, already a global icon, showcased his brilliance on the pitch, despite Brazil's disappointing quarterfinal exit.

Their meeting during the group stage left an indelible mark on the tournament. Portugal stunned Brazil with a 3-1 victory, with Eusebio scoring twice.

The mutual respect and admiration between Eusebio and Pelé served as a reminder of football's ability to bring players together, even amidst intense competition.

F. Dalglish vs. Rush: Liverpool's Dynamic Duo

In the 1980s, Liverpool's Scottish wizard Kenny Dalglish and Welsh goal-machine Ian Rush formed a legendary partnership, terrorizing opposition defenses and propelling Liverpool to domestic and European success.

Dalglish, known for his sublime skill and creative playmaking, was the orchestrator of Liverpool's attacks. Rush, on the other hand, possessed lethal finishing ability, making him one of the most feared strikers of his generation.

Their rivalry with other clubs was intense, but together, they formed a formidable duo, leading Liverpool to several league titles and European triumphs.

Their partnership showcased the beauty of collaboration on the football pitch, where individual brilliance can combine to create something truly extraordinary.

G. Best vs. Charlton: Manchester United's Icons

George Best and Bobby Charlton were two of Manchester United's most celebrated players, each leaving a lasting legacy at the club.

Best, the Northern Irish maverick, was renowned for his dazzling dribbling, incredible balance, and ability to score from improbable situations.

Charlton, the English midfielder, was a complete player with a thunderous long-range shot and a keen footballing intelligence.

Their rivalry was not of the antagonistic kind, but rather a friendly competition to excel on the pitch and elevate Manchester United to greater heights.

Their presence at Manchester United during the 1960s and 1970s was instrumental in shaping the club's identity and global reputation.

H. <u>Gerrard vs. Lampard: The Battle of Midfield Maestros</u>

Steven Gerrard and Frank Lampard were two of England's finest midfielders of their generation.

Their rivalry was not limited to the intense competition between Liverpool and Chelsea in the Premier League, but also extended to the international stage.

Gerrard, the talismanic captain of Liverpool, was known for his powerful long-range strikes, impeccable passing, and leadership on the pitch. Lampard, the dynamic midfielder of Chelsea, possessed incredible goal-scoring instincts, making him one of the highest-scoring midfielders in Premier League history.

Their rivalry reached its peak during England's campaigns in major tournaments.

As they both vied for the central midfield position, fans and pundits debated over who was the better player.

Despite their club allegiances, Gerrard and Lampard shared a mutual respect for each other's abilities.

Both players recognized the qualities that made them unique and understood the challenges of being midfield leaders for their respective teams.

Their rivalry serves as a reminder of how individual brilliance can coexist with respect and camaraderie, as Gerrard and Lampard showcased the best of English midfield talent during their careers.

Chapter 5: Quirky Anecdotes about Football Legends

5.1 *The Superstitions of Football Icons: Lucky Charms and Rituals*

Football is a sport rich in traditions and superstitions, and even the most talented and celebrated players are not immune to the allure of lucky charms and pre-match rituals.

From wearing specific garments to performing certain routines, football icons have embraced superstitions as a way to boost their confidence and enhance their performance on the pitch. In this section, we explore the fascinating world of the superstitions of football icons, uncovering the quirky rituals that have become an integral part of their pre-match routines.

A. **Cristiano Ronaldo's Pre-Match Leap:**

Cristiano Ronaldo, one of the most superstitious players in football, has a well-known pre-match ritual that involves a high leap before kick-off.

As the camera pans to him in the tunnel, fans often witness Ronaldo taking a massive leap into the air before stepping onto the pitch.

The leap is believed to be a way for Ronaldo to release nervous energy and symbolize his readiness for the game ahead. It has become an iconic image associated with the Portuguese superstar, and he continues to perform the ritual before every match.

B. <u>Francesco Totti's Turnaround Trick:</u>

Francesco Totti, the legendary Italian forward who spent his entire career at AS Roma, had a quirky pre-match ritual that became a trademark of his personality on the pitch.

Before taking his position on the field for kick-off, Totti would turn around three times.

The ritual was often accompanied by a cheeky grin, endearing him even more to the Roma faithful.

The exact reason behind Totti's turnaround trick remains a mystery, but it is believed to be a way for him to channel focus and energy before the match.

C. <u>Sergio Goycochea's Bathroom Routine:</u>

Sergio Goycochea, the Argentine goalkeeper who became a penalty-saving hero in the 1990 FIFA World Cup, had a peculiar pre-match ritual involving the bathroom.

Before penalty shootouts, Goycochea would retreat to the bathroom and wash his hands repeatedly. He believed that this ritual brought him luck and helped him stay calm during high-pressure moments.

His belief in the bathroom routine seemed to work, as he made several crucial penalty saves that propelled Argentina to the World Cup final.

D. Juan Roman Riquelme's Gum-Chewing Habit:

Juan Roman Riquelme, the Argentine playmaker known for his exquisite passing and vision, had a distinctive gum-chewing habit on the pitch. Throughout his career, Riquelme was rarely seen without a piece of gum in his mouth during games.

He believed that chewing gum helped him stay relaxed and focused on the pitch, allowing him to maintain a calm and composed demeanor even in high-pressure situations.

The gum-chewing ritual became a signature feature of Riquelme's playing style and added to his aura of composure and control on the field.

E. Hakan Şükür's Lucky Number 11:

Hakan Şükür, the Turkish striker known for his goal-scoring exploits, had a superstition involving the number 11.

Throughout his career, Şükür wore the number 11 jersey for both club and country.

He considered the number 11 to be his lucky charm and believed that it brought him good fortune on the pitch.

The number 11 became synonymous with Şükür's goal-scoring prowess, and he remains one of Turkey's all-time leading goal-scorers.

5.2 _Famous Players Who Nearly Chose Different Career Paths_

Behind every successful football player lies a journey of tough decisions and pivotal moments that shaped their destiny on the pitch. While we celebrate the accomplishments of these famous players, it's fascinating to delve into the alternate paths they might have taken if not for a twist of fate. In this section, we explore the stories of renowned footballers who came close to pursuing different career paths, revealing the near-miss scenarios that could have dramatically altered the course of football history.

A. **Zlatan Ibrahimović - From Bike Racer to Football Icon:**

Zlatan Ibrahimović, the enigmatic Swedish striker known for his acrobatic goals and towering presence, initially had dreams of becoming a professional bike racer.

Growing up in Sweden, Ibrahimović was an avid cyclist and even participated in local races.

However, his passion for football soon took over, and he decided to pursue a career in the sport.

It turned out to be a fortuitous choice, as Ibrahimović went on to achieve success with some of Europe's biggest clubs and solidified his status as one of football's most charismatic and dominant figures.

B. <u>Manuel Neuer - The Young Drummer's Dilemma:</u>

Manuel Neuer, the German goalkeeper revered for his shot-stopping abilities and distribution skills, had a tough choice to make in his youth – pursue a career in music or football.

As a talented drummer, Neuer faced the decision of joining a music academy to hone his skills.

Ultimately, his love for football prevailed, and he decided to dedicate himself to the beautiful game.

The world of football can thank Neuer's decision, as he went on to become one of the best goalkeepers in history and played a crucial role in Germany's 2014 FIFA World Cup victory.

C. <u>Andrea Pirlo - The Restaurant Business vs. Midfield Maestro:</u>

Andrea Pirlo, the Italian midfield maestro known for his elegance and vision, contemplated an entirely different career path before football beckoned.

During his early years, Pirlo had a keen interest in the restaurant business and seriously considered becoming a chef.

However, his footballing talent was evident, and he ultimately chose to pursue a career on the pitch. Pirlo's decision paid off handsomely, as he enjoyed a decorated career at clubs like AC Milan and Juventus, winning numerous domestic and international titles, including the FIFA World Cup with Italy in 2006.

D. <u>Harry Kane - The Aspiring NFL Punter:</u>

Before becoming one of England's most prolific strikers, Harry Kane, the Tottenham Hotspur and England goal machine, considered a career in American football.

As a teenager, Kane was an accomplished soccer player but also showed promise as a kicker in American football.

He even attended a few training camps in the United States, trying his hand at punting.

In the end, Kane chose to stay true to his first love, soccer, and focused on making a name for himself in the sport.

His decision proved to be a wise one, as he evolved into one of the most lethal strikers in the world, earning Golden Boot awards and leading England's attack on the international stage.

E. Luka Modrić - The Troubadour on the Field:

Luka Modrić, the Croatian midfield maestro and captain of the national team, has a passion for singing and playing the guitar that could have led him to a career in music.

Throughout his life, Modrić has enjoyed performing as a singer and guitarist, and he has even showcased his musical talents at various events.

However, his love for football and remarkable skills on the pitch guided him towards a career in sports. Modrić's footballing journey led him to win prestigious honors with clubs like Tottenham Hotspur and Real Madrid, as well as leading Croatia to the FIFA World Cup Final in 2018.

5.3 *Legends' Nicknames: How Football Heroes Earned Their Monikers*

In the world of football, iconic players often acquire unique and memorable nicknames that reflect their playing style, personality, or extraordinary abilities on the pitch.

These monikers become an integral part of their legacy, with fans and fellow players affectionately using them to refer to their football heroes.

In this section, we delve into the intriguing origins of some of football's most famous player nicknames, shedding light on the stories behind these endearing titles.

A. "The Divine Ponytail" - Roberto Baggio:

Roberto Baggio, the Italian forward known for his flowing ponytail and majestic playing style, acquired the nickname "The Divine Ponytail" during his illustrious career.

His elegance, flair, and creativity on the ball earned him this affectionate title, which remains synonymous with his legacy as one of Italy's finest footballers.

B. "Captain Tsubasa" - Hidetoshi Nakata:

Hidetoshi Nakata, the Japanese midfield maestro, earned the nickname "Captain Tsubasa" due to his striking resemblance to the popular manga and anime character of the same name.

Nakata was known for his elegance on the ball and was a trailblazer for Asian players in European football.

C. "The Kaiser" - Franz Beckenbauer:

Franz Beckenbauer, the German footballing legend and World Cup winner, earned the nickname "The Kaiser" due to his commanding presence and regal demeanor on the pitch.

His leadership skills and vision as a defender made him one of the most influential players in the history of the game.

D. "The Flying Dutchman" - Dennis Bergkamp:

Dennis Bergkamp, the Dutch forward known for his graceful movement and exquisite skill, acquired the nickname "The Flying Dutchman" due to his ability to glide past defenders with ease.

His technical brilliance and penchant for scoring spectacular goals made him a revered figure in both Dutch and Arsenal footballing history.

E. "The Baby-Faced Assassin" - Ole Gunnar Solskjær:

Ole Gunnar Solskjær, the Norwegian striker known for his clinical finishing and memorable late goals, acquired the nickname "The Baby-Faced Assassin" during his time at Manchester United.

Solskjær's youthful appearance, combined with his lethal ability to score crucial goals as a super-sub, earned him the moniker.

He was often called upon from the bench to rescue matches for Manchester United, leaving opponents stunned like a silent assassin.

F. "The Ginger Wizard" - Matt Le Tissier:

Matt Le Tissier, the Southampton and England midfielder, earned the nickname "The Ginger Wizard" due to his red hair and magical footballing abilities.

Le Tissier was known for his incredible skill on the ball, including his ability to score breathtaking goals from long range and his remarkable success rate from penalties.

His loyalty to Southampton throughout his career made him a beloved figure among the club's fans.

Chapter 6: Unknown Players Suddenly Thrust into the Spotlight

6.1 *From Amateur to Hero: Players Who Rose to Fame Overnight*

In the world of football, fairy-tale stories often unfold, where seemingly ordinary players rise from obscurity to become overnight heroes. These players, who once plied their trade in amateur leagues or lower divisions, experienced a meteoric ascent to fame and glory, captivating the hearts of football fans worldwide. In this section, we explore the inspiring journeys of some of these remarkable individuals who transformed from amateurs into celebrated stars.

A. Jamie Vardy - The Non-League Sensation:

Jamie Vardy's rise from playing in the non-league football system to becoming a Premier League champion with Leicester City is one of football's most extraordinary tales.

Born in Sheffield, England, Vardy struggled to secure a professional contract in his early career and found himself playing in the lower echelons of English football.

His breakthrough came in the 2011-2012 season when he joined Fleetwood Town. Vardy's blistering pace, tenacity, and clinical finishing caught the attention of scouts, and Leicester City signed him in 2012. His impact on the Premier League was immense, and he played a pivotal role in Leicester's historic title-winning campaign during the 2015-2016 season.

B. Riyad Mahrez - From the French Lower Divisions to Premier League Glory:

Riyad Mahrez's journey from the French lower divisions to becoming a Premier League champion with Leicester City mirrors Vardy's fairy-tale ascent. Born in Algeria, Mahrez honed his skills in the lower divisions of French football, playing for clubs like Quimper and Le Havre.

In 2014, Leicester City signed Mahrez, and he quickly showcased his exceptional dribbling ability, flair, and eye for goal.

His contributions were instrumental in Leicester's remarkable title triumph, and Mahrez's performances earned him widespread recognition and accolades.

C. <u>Michu - The Swansea City Revelation:</u>

Michu, a Spanish attacking midfielder, experienced a sensational rise to fame during his time at Swansea City in the Premier League.

Before joining Swansea in 2012, Michu played for clubs in Spain, including Rayo Vallecano and Celta Vigo, without attracting significant attention.

Upon arriving in Wales, Michu's goal-scoring prowess took the Premier League by storm.

He scored 18 goals in his debut season for Swansea, earning him a reputation as one of the league's most clinical finishers.

His impact on the team was immense, guiding Swansea to a historic League Cup victory in 2013.

D. <u>Ole Gunnar Solskjær - The Super-Sub Sensation:</u>

Ole Gunnar Solskjær, the Norwegian striker, etched his name in Manchester United folklore with his incredible impact as a super-substitute.

Before joining Manchester United in 1996, Solskjær played for Norwegian club Molde.

At United, Solskjær's ability to score crucial goals off the bench became legendary. He earned the nickname "The Baby-Faced Assassin" for his habit of scoring late and decisive goals, which often rescued the team from difficult situations.

His most famous moment came in the 1999 UEFA Champions League final, where his last-minute goal secured United's historic treble.

E. Davor Šuker - From the Croatian Leagues to World Cup Golden Boot:

Davor Šuker, the Croatian striker, rose to prominence in the 1990s, guiding Croatia to the semi-finals of the 1998 FIFA World Cup.

Before joining European giants like Sevilla and Real Madrid, Šuker played for clubs in Croatia, including Hajduk Split and Dinamo Zagreb.

In the 1998 World Cup, Šuker's clinical finishing and goal-scoring prowess earned him the Golden Boot as the tournament's top scorer.

His performances played a significant role in Croatia's historic World Cup run, cementing his status as one of his country's greatest footballers.

6.2 *Cinderella Stories: Football's Unlikely Heroes in Key Matches*

Football's allure lies in its ability to produce mesmerizing moments of magic and unexpected heroes. In crucial matches, when the stakes are at their highest, football has seen the emergence of unlikely heroes who etched their names in history with their awe-inspiring performances.

These Cinderella stories showcase the power of determination, belief, and the ability to rise to the occasion when the odds are stacked against them. In this section, we explore some of football's most remarkable Cinderella stories featuring unlikely heroes in key matches.

A. Lars Ricken - UEFA Champions League Final, 1997:

In the 1997 UEFA Champions League final between Borussia Dortmund and Juventus, an 18-year-old Lars Ricken etched his name in football folklore.

With Dortmund leading 2-1, Ricken came on as a substitute in the 71st minute.

Just 16 seconds after stepping onto the pitch, he received a long-range pass from teammate Andreas Möller and delicately lobbed the ball over Juventus goalkeeper Angelo Peruzzi, sealing a 3-1 victory for Dortmund.

Ricken's goal made him the youngest scorer in a Champions League final and exemplified the magic of football's unexpected heroes.

B. <u>Didier Drogba - UEFA Champions League Final, 2012:</u>

In the 2012 UEFA Champions League final between Chelsea and Bayern Munich, Didier Drogba, the Ivorian striker, produced a heroic performance when it mattered most.

With Chelsea trailing 1-0 in the dying minutes of regulation time, Drogba rose above Bayern's defense to head home a dramatic equalizer, sending the match into extra time. In the penalty shootout, Drogba demonstrated nerves of steel, slotting home the decisive penalty to give Chelsea their first-ever Champions League title.

His impact in the final showcased the influence of a true big-game player.

C. <u>Maxi Rodríguez - FIFA World Cup Round of 16, 2006:</u>

In the 2006 FIFA World Cup Round of 16 match between Argentina and Mexico, Maxi Rodríguez, the

Argentine midfielder, provided a moment of pure magic.

With the score tied at 1-1 in extra time, Rodríguez unleashed an incredible volley from outside the box, sending the ball crashing into the top corner of the net.

His stunning strike secured a 2-1 victory for Argentina and remains one of the most memorable goals in World Cup history.

D. <u>Paul Caligiuri - FIFA World Cup Qualifier, 1989:</u>

In a crucial FIFA World Cup qualifier between the United States and Trinidad and Tobago in 1989, Paul Caligiuri, the American midfielder, produced a moment of brilliance that altered the course of U.S. soccer history.

With the match tied at 0-0, Caligiuri unleashed a powerful long-range shot that found the back of the net, securing a 1-0 victory for the United States and propelling them to the 1990 FIFA World Cup, their first appearance in the tournament since 1950.

E. <u>Geoff Hurst - FIFA World Cup Final, 1966:</u>

In the 1966 FIFA World Cup final between England and West Germany, Geoff Hurst, the English striker, had the game of a lifetime.

With the match tied at 2-2 in extra time, Hurst completed his hat-trick in dramatic fashion, striking the ball with power and precision, and the ball hit the underside of the crossbar before bouncing over the line.

This iconic moment is famously known as the "Wembley Goal" and remains the only hat-trick scored in a World Cup final.

F. <u>Toto Schillaci - FIFA World Cup, 1990:</u>

During the 1990 FIFA World Cup held in Italy, Salvatore "Toto" Schillaci became a national hero by leading the Italian national team to an unexpected third-place finish.

Schillaci, a relatively unknown striker before the tournament, burst onto the scene with his goal-scoring prowess.

He scored six goals in the tournament, winning the Golden Boot as the top scorer.

His goals and infectious enthusiasm endeared him to the Italian fans, making him an unlikely hero in Italy's successful World Cup campaign.

Chapter 7: The Most Incredible and Unusual Records in Football

7.1 *Unbeatable Defenses: Longest Clean Sheets and Defensive Records*

In football, defense is an art form, and teams that boast impenetrable defenses often leave a lasting legacy.

The ability to keep clean sheets and set defensive records showcases the resilience, organization, and discipline of a team's backline and goalkeeper.

In this section, we delve into some of the most remarkable defensive records and longest clean sheet streaks in football history, highlighting the accomplishments of teams that mastered the art of defending.

A. AC Milan's Rock-Solid Defense (1993-1994):

During the 1993-1994 Serie A season, AC Milan displayed defensive prowess that cemented their status as one of Italy's greatest teams. Under the guidance of coach Fabio Capello, Milan set a remarkable record by going unbeaten for 58 consecutive league matches. This astonishing feat remains unparalleled in Italian football history.

Led by the likes of Franco Baresi, Paolo Maldini, and Alessandro Costacurta, Milan's defense was virtually impenetrable, conceding just 15 goals in the entire 1993-1994 season.

Their remarkable defensive stability propelled them to the Serie A title, marking an era of dominance for the Rossoneri.

B. Chelsea's "Blue Wall" (2004-2005):

Under the management of José Mourinho, Chelsea established themselves as a defensive force to be reckoned with during the 2004-2005 Premier League season.

The team's defensive solidity was epitomized by a record-breaking 1,025 minutes without conceding a goal in the league, setting a new English top-flight record.

The "Blue Wall" was built on the defensive partnership of John Terry and Ricardo Carvalho, with Claude Makélélé providing a formidable shield in front of the defense.

Chelsea's defensive prowess played a pivotal role in securing their first Premier League title in 50 years.

C. Bayern Munich's Defensive Wall (2012-2013):

During the 2012-2013 Bundesliga season, Bayern Munich's defense, led by coach Jupp Heynckes, was an impenetrable force.

The team set a new Bundesliga record by conceding just 18 goals in the entire league campaign.

The central defensive partnership of Jerome Boateng and Dante proved to be rock-solid, with goalkeeper Manuel Neuer offering a commanding presence between the posts.

Bayern's defensive excellence culminated in winning the Bundesliga title and the UEFA Champions League, cementing their status as one of Europe's finest teams.

D. Italy's Sturdy Backline in the 2006 FIFA World Cup:

The Italian national team showcased their defensive prowess during the 2006 FIFA World Cup, where they famously adopted the tactical system known as "Catenaccio."

Led by captain Fabio Cannavaro, Italy's defense was disciplined, organized, and resolute.

Over the course of the tournament, Italy conceded just two goals in regular play, boasting a mean and unyielding defense.

This defensive masterclass culminated in Italy winning the World Cup, with their defensive solidity being the backbone of their success.

E. Darije Kalezic's Dutch Defensive Record (1989-1990):

Darije Kalezić, a Bosnian-Dutch footballer, etched his name in Dutch football history during the 1989-1990 Eredivisie season while playing for NAC Breda.

Kalezić set a remarkable individual record by going 1,196 minutes without conceding a goal, setting a new record for the longest clean sheet streak in Dutch football.

Kalezić's unwavering performances in goal and his ability to keep opponents at bay played a crucial role in NAC Breda's defensive excellence that season. His record-breaking feat remains a testament to the impact of a resolute goalkeeper on a team's defensive success.

F. Greece's Defensive Heroics in EURO 2004:

During the 2004 UEFA European Championship, Greece, under coach Otto Rehhagel, produced one of the greatest underdog stories in football history.

The Greek national team executed a disciplined and robust defensive strategy, dubbed "Rehhagel's Wall." Throughout the tournament, Greece's defense, led by the likes of Traianos Dellas and Angelos Basinas, frustrated opponents and conceded just four goals in total.

In the final against Portugal, Greece's defense held strong, and they secured a famous 1-0 victory to claim their first-ever major international trophy.

7.2 *Record-Breaking Goals: Strikers Who Rewrote the History Books*

In the world of football, goal-scoring is an art form, and the players who rewrite the history books with their goal-scoring exploits are celebrated as legends. From domestic leagues to international competitions, these prolific strikers leave an indelible mark on the sport and become synonymous with goal-scoring greatness.

In this section, we delve into the journeys of some of the most prolific goal-scorers who have set record-breaking feats and left an enduring legacy in football.

A. Josef Bican - The Unrivaled Goal Machine:

Austrian-Czech forward Josef Bican is arguably the most prolific goal-scorer in football history. Playing during the mid-20th century, Bican set remarkable records that still stand to this day.

He scored a staggering 805 official goals in just 530 matches, an astonishing goal-scoring ratio that has never been matched.

Bican's goal-scoring prowess was not limited to domestic football; he also scored 14 goals in 19 appearances for the Czechoslovakia national team. His ability to find the back of the net with ease and his knack for setting goal-scoring records make him an all-time great in the history of the sport.

B. <u>Pelé - The Brazilian Goal-Scoring Phenomenon:</u>

Edson Arantes do Nascimento, popularly known as Pelé, is widely regarded as one of the greatest footballers of all time.
The Brazilian forward's goal-scoring exploits are legendary, and he holds several remarkable records.
Pelé scored an incredible 1,281 goals in 1,363 official matches during his illustrious career.
His ability to score with both feet and his exceptional heading ability made him a goal-scoring phenomenon.
Pelé's contributions led Brazil to three FIFA World Cup titles, and he remains a symbol of footballing greatness around the world.

C. <u>Gerd Müller - Der Bomber of Bayern Munich:</u>

Gerd Müller, nicknamed "Der Bomber," was a German forward known for his lethal goal-scoring instincts. During his time at Bayern Munich, Müller was a goal-scoring machine, terrorizing opposition defenses with his clinical finishing.

Müller's most notable record came during the 1971-1972 Bundesliga season when he scored an astonishing 40 league goals.

That record stood for 49 years until it was surpassed by Robert Lewandowski in the 2020-2021 season. Müller's goal-scoring prowess and his 365 league goals for Bayern Munich established him as one of the greatest goal-scorers in the history of German football.

D. <u>Cristiano Ronaldo - The Modern-Day Goal-Scoring Phenom:</u>

Portuguese forward Cristiano Ronaldo is a modern-day goal-scoring phenomenon who has set numerous records in the 21st century.

Ronaldo's goal-scoring journey started at Sporting Lisbon and continued at Manchester United, Real Madrid, Juventus, and later, his return to Manchester United.

Ronaldo's goal-scoring prowess is characterized by his incredible athleticism, goal-scoring instincts, and versatility.

He holds records for the most goals scored in UEFA Champions League history, the most hat-tricks in La Liga, and the most goals in UEFA European Championship history.

Cristiano Ronaldo had scored over 839 goals (update in 06/2023) in his career, firmly establishing himself as one of the greatest goal-scorers of all time and a modern football legend.

E. Lionel Messi - The Maestro of Barcelona:

Argentine forward Lionel Messi is another modern-day goal-scoring maestro who has redefined what is possible on a football pitch.

Messi spent the majority of his career at Barcelona, where he became the club's all-time leading goal-scorer and set multiple records.

Messi's low center of gravity, close ball control, and lethal left foot make him a goal-scoring threat from almost any position on the field. He has won numerous individual awards, including multiple Ballon d'Or titles, and holds records for the most goals scored in a calendar year and the most goals scored for a single club.

As of my knowledge cutoff in September 2021, Lionel Messi had scored 806 goals in his career (update in 06/2023) and continues to mesmerize football fans around the world with his goal-scoring brilliance.

F. Ferenc Puskás - The Galloping Major:

Hungarian forward Ferenc Puskás, known as the "Galloping Major," was a legendary goal-scorer during the 1950s and 1960s. Puskás had a remarkable goal-scoring record at both club level, notably with Real Madrid, and for the Hungary national team.

With Real Madrid, Puskás won numerous La Liga titles and five consecutive European Cups, establishing the club as a dominant force in European football.

His partnership with Alfredo Di Stéfano was one of the most formidable attacking duos of their time.

Puskás also led the Hungary national team to great success, notably reaching the final of the 1954 FIFA World Cup.

His goal-scoring exploits and technical prowess continue to inspire footballers worldwide.

7.3 *The list of 10 highest-scoring football matches in history:*

1. AS Adema 149–0 Stade Olympique L'Emyrne (October 31, 2002) - This match in Madagascar's THB Champions League set a record for the most one-sided match in football history. Stade Olympique L'Emyrne deliberately scored own goals to protest against refereeing decisions.
2. Australia 31–0 American Samoa (April 11, 2001) - In a FIFA World Cup qualifier, Australia secured a resounding victory, setting a record for the highest-scoring international match.
3. Dinamo Bucureşti 11–0 Ştiinţa Bacău (April 17, 1977) - In a Romanian league match, Dinamo Bucureşti achieved a dominant victory.
4. Arbroath 36–0 Bon Accord (September 12, 1885) - In a Scottish Cup match, Arbroath set a record for the highest-scoring match in British senior football.
5. Tottenham Hotspur 13–2 Crewe Alexandra (February 3, 1960) - This FA Cup match remains one of the highest-scoring matches in English football history.
6. Celtic 13–0 East Kilbride (January 21, 2017) - Celtic's dominant victory in the Scottish Cup set a modern record for the club.

7. Manchester United 9–0 Ipswich Town (March 4, 1995) - Manchester United's emphatic victory in the Premier League remains one of the highest-scoring matches in the league's history.
8. Manchester United 9–0 Southampton (February 2, 2021) - In a Premier League fixture, Manchester United equalled their own record for the highest-scoring match in the league.
9. Real Madrid 8–2 Deportivo La Coruña (September 20, 2014) - In a La Liga match, Real Madrid secured a dominant victory.
10. Chelsea 8–0 Wigan Athletic (May 9, 2010) - Chelsea's emphatic victory on the final day of the Premier League season helped secure the league title.

7.4 _Teams never relegated in "2nd division_

- **Premier League (England):** No team
- **La Liga (Spain):** Barcelona, Real Madrid, Athletic Bilbao
- **Bundesliga (Germany):** No team
- **Serie A (Italy):** FC Internazionale
- **Ligue 1 (France):** No team
- **Eredivisie (Netherlands):** Ajax, PSV Eindhoven, Feyenoord, Utrecht
- **Primeira Liga (Portugal):** Benfica, FC Porto, Sporting Lisbon
- **Scottish Premiership (Scotland):** Celtic, Aberdeen
- **Süper Lig (Turkey):** Fenerbahce, Galatasaray e Besiktas
- **Prem"jer-liha (Ukraine):** Dinamo Kiev
- **Prem'er-Liga (Russia):** CSKA Moscow, Spartak Moscow, Lokomotiv Moscow
- **Souper Ligka Ellada (Greece):** Olympiakos, Panathinaikos, PAOK
- **Primera División argentina (Argentina):** Boca Juniors
- **Campeonato Brasileiro Série A (Brazil):** Flamengo, Santos, Sao Paulo, Cruzeiro
- **Primera División (Chile): Colo Colo**

7.5 *The youngest rookie in history*

Mauricio Baldivieso was born on September 20, 2004, in Santa Cruz de la Sierra, Bolivia.

He made his professional debut in Bolivian football at the incredibly young age of 12 years and 300 days.

The debut took place on July 18, 2017, when he played for Oriente Petrolero, a Bolivian Primera División team, in the match against Club Universitario de Sucre.

7.6 *The game with the most spectators in football history*

The game with the highest number of spectators in football history took place during the 1950 FIFA World Cup held in Brazil.

The match was the final game of the tournament, known as the "Maracanazo," and it was played on July 16, 1950, at the Maracanã Stadium in Rio de Janeiro, Brazil.

The final match of the 1950 World Cup was contested between Brazil and Uruguay.

The Maracanã Stadium, which was built specifically for the tournament and designed to hold a massive crowd, was packed to its full capacity.

The official attendance for the game was recorded as approximately 199,854 spectators.

The atmosphere in the stadium was electrifying, with passionate Brazilian fans expecting their team to claim the title on home soil.

However, the match ended in a shocking upset, as Uruguay won 2-1, thus earning their second World Cup title. The defeat was a devastating blow for the host nation, and the term "Maracanazo" has since been used to refer to this historic match and its unexpected outcome.

The Maracanã Stadium remains an iconic venue in football history, hosting numerous memorable matches and events. While the stadium's capacity has been reduced since its initial construction due to safety regulations, it continues to be one of the most revered football arenas in the world.

It's essential to note that the Maracanã Stadium's official capacity has been adjusted over the years, and the attendance figures for some historic matches, including the 1950 World Cup final, have been a subject of debate. Nevertheless, the 1950 World Cup final remains one of the most significant football events in history, attracting an enormous crowd and leaving a lasting impact on the sport's legacy in Brazil and beyond.

7.7 *The oldest football team in history*

The oldest football team in history is a matter of some debate, as the origins of football can be traced back to various periods and locations. However, one of the oldest football clubs that still exists and has a documented history is Sheffield Football Club, often referred to as Sheffield FC.

Sheffield FC was founded on October 24, 1857, in Sheffield, England.

It is widely recognized as the world's oldest football club with continuous existence. The club was established by Nathaniel Creswick and William Prest, who were former students of the Sheffield Collegiate School.

They formalized a set of rules for their football matches, which eventually evolved into the modern-day rules of the game.

Sheffield FC played its early matches according to its own set of rules, which were different from the standardized rules used today. As the sport of football began to spread, various clubs adopted different rule sets, leading to some variations in how the game was played.

While Sheffield FC holds the distinction of being one of the oldest football clubs with an unbroken history, there were other teams and informal football matches that took place before its establishment.

These early matches were often disorganized and lacked formal club structures.

Aside from Sheffield FC, there are other historical football clubs that claim to be among the oldest, such as Hallam FC, also based in Sheffield, which was founded in 1860.

Both Sheffield FC and Hallam FC have played an essential role in the development and popularization of football in its early years.

Chapter 8: Incidents and Bizarre Moments on the Field

8.1 *Football's Most Bizarre Goals: From Unintentional Flukes to Golazos*

A. The "Beckham's Goal from the Halfway Line":

One of the most iconic bizarre goals in football history was scored by none other than David Beckham himself. On August 17, 1996, while playing for Manchester United, Beckham spotted Wimbledon's goalkeeper, Neil Sullivan, off his line.
Seizing the opportunity, Beckham launched a precise lob from the halfway line that sailed over the stranded goalkeeper and nestled into the net.
The audacious strike earned Beckham international fame and set a new benchmark for long-range goals.

B. The "Olimpico" Corner Kick:

Scoring directly from a corner kick, known as an "olimpico," is a rare and extraordinary feat. However, some players have managed to achieve this improbable goal. One such memorable instance was during the 2014 FIFA World Cup when Brazilian superstar Neymar curled a corner kick that baffled the Croatian defense and nestled into the far corner of the net. The olimpico goal showcased Neymar's exceptional technique and precision.

C. The "Beach Ball Goal":

In a Premier League clash between Liverpool and Sunderland in October 2009, a bizarre incident unfolded that saw a beach ball play a pivotal role in the match.
As a Liverpool player struck the ball, it deflected off a beach ball that had made its way onto the pitch, completely confusing the Sunderland goalkeeper.
The ball found the back of the net, leading to a controversial and unforgettable goal.

D. The "Backheel Golazo":

Football fans adore a well-executed backheel goal, but one particular backheel golazo left spectators stunned. In a match between Sweden and England in 2012, Swedish striker Zlatan Ibrahimović scored one of the greatest goals ever witnessed. From an impossible angle, Ibrahimović launched himself into the air and performed a perfect backheel that looped over the goalkeeper and into the net. The goal showcased Ibrahimović's ingenuity and skill in the most extraordinary way.

E. The "Escaped Pigeon Goal":

In a Dutch Eredivisie match between AZ Alkmaar and FC Twente in 2010, a peculiar incident occurred when a pigeon found its way onto the pitch. As the ball was crossed into the penalty area, the pigeon accidentally deflected the ball into the net with its wings. The goal was allowed to stand, and the unexpected contribution from the feathered intruder became a memorable moment in football history.

F. The "Goalkeeper's Long-Distance Strike":

Goalkeepers are known for their shot-stopping abilities, but sometimes they surprise everyone with their scoring prowess.

In a match between Middlesbrough and Manchester City in 2004, Middlesbrough goalkeeper Mark Schwarzer ventured forward for a corner kick in the dying moments of the game. Astonishingly, the ball fell to Schwarzer outside the box, and he smashed a powerful shot into the net to earn his team an unlikely point.

G. The "Rabona Penalty Kick":

Penalty kicks are typically straightforward, but some players opt for unconventional techniques to confuse the goalkeeper. In a Chilean Primera División match in 2016, Universidad de Chile's Felipe Mora took a penalty using the "rabona" technique, wrapping his non-dominant leg around his standing leg to strike the ball. The goal left the goalkeeper rooted to the spot and showcased Mora's creativity in the heat of the moment.

8.2 Controversial Celebrations:Memorable Acts and Red Cards

In the passionate and emotionally charged world of football, celebrations are an integral part of the game. They are moments of unbridled joy and camaraderie shared between players and fans alike. However, not all celebrations are met with approval, as some have sparked controversy and even resulted in red cards. From exuberant displays of emotion to provocative gestures, controversial celebrations have left an indelible mark on the sport's history. Let's delve into some memorable acts that caused a stir on and off the pitch.

A. The "Shirtless Slide" - Brandi Chastain (USA):

Brandi Chastain's "shirtless slide" celebration is one of the most iconic and memorable moments in women's football history. It took place during the 1999 FIFA Women's World Cup final between the United States and China, held at the Rose Bowl in Pasadena, California.

The final match was a tense and closely contested affair, with neither team able to score during regulation time and extra time. The fate of the World Cup would be decided by a penalty shootout.

As the penalty shootout unfolded, the pressure was palpable.

The United States and China exchanged successful penalties, but it was Chastain's moment that would become etched in football lore. In the fifth round of penalties, Chastain stepped up to take her shot with a chance to secure victory for her team.

With nerves of steel, Chastain struck the ball with precision, sending it into the back of the net and securing the World Cup title for the United States.

The sheer exhilaration and relief of the moment were evident on her face as she tore off her jersey in celebration, revealing a black sports bra underneath.

In a moment of pure exuberance and joy, Chastain dropped to her knees and slid across the field on the grass, arms raised in triumph.

Her emotional and spontaneous celebration captured the elation and determination of the U.S. team and the significance of their victory in front of a home crowd.

The image of Chastain in her sports bra, celebrating with her arms outstretched, became an iconic representation of women's football and the growth of the sport in the United States. It symbolized the passion, dedication, and skill of the female athletes who had worked tirelessly to elevate women's football to new heights.

Chastain's celebration resonated beyond the football field and became a powerful symbol of empowerment for women and girls around the world. It inspired a generation of young female athletes and helped raise awareness and support for women's football globally. Beyond her celebration, Brandi Chastain's impact on women's football extended far beyond the 1999 World Cup. She was a pioneer for women's sports and a vocal advocate for gender equality in athletics.

Her remarkable career and influential contributions continue to inspire future generations of female footballers and athletes celebration, revealing her sports bra.

The iconic image of her triumphant moment became an enduring symbol of women's soccer and inspired a new generation of female athletes.

B. The "Kung Fu Kick" - Eric Cantona (Manchester United):

Eric Cantona's "kung fu kick" is one of the most infamous incidents in football history, forever etched in the minds of football fans around the world. The incident occurred on January 25, 1995, during a Premier League match between Manchester United and Crystal Palace at Selhurst Park.

During the game, Cantona was involved in a heated exchange with Crystal Palace defender Richard Shaw. After being fouled, Cantona responded with a retaliatory kick towards Shaw. As if the kick itself wasn't shocking enough, what followed was even more astonishing. Cantona launched himself into the crowd with a flying kick directed at a Crystal Palace supporter, Matthew Simmons, who had been taunting him.

The incident triggered chaos on the pitch, with players and officials rushing to separate Cantona from the crowd. He was subsequently shown a red card and sent off, leaving Manchester United with only ten men for the remainder of the match.

Cantona's actions were met with widespread condemnation from the footballing world. He faced severe repercussions from both the Football Association (FA) and Manchester United. The FA handed him a nine-month ban from all football-related activities, which effectively ruled him out for the rest of the season. Manchester United also imposed their own punishment, extending his suspension for an additional four months and fining him heavily.

The incident tarnished Cantona's reputation, but it also highlighted the intensity and pressure that professional footballers face both on and off the pitch. It also sparked discussions about the conduct of players and the behavior of fans in football stadiums.

Despite the controversy, Cantona returned to football and continued to excel for Manchester United, playing a crucial role in their success during the mid-1990s. Over time, he earned redemption in the eyes of many fans and is now celebrated as one of the most iconic players in Manchester United's history.

While the "kung fu kick" remains a dark moment in Cantona's career, it also serves as a reminder of the complexities of the beautiful game and the emotions that can sometimes boil over in the heat of competition.

C. The "Finger Gesture" - Paolo Di Canio (Lazio):

Paolo Di Canio's "finger gesture" is one of the most controversial and widely discussed incidents in football history. The incident occurred during a Serie A match between Lazio and AS Roma on January 6, 2000, when Di Canio played as a forward for Lazio.

During the match, tensions were high between the players on both sides.

The altercation escalated, and Di Canio directed a fascist salute towards Lazio's hardcore supporters, known as "ultras," during a corner kick.

The gesture involved raising his right arm, palm down, and making an extended straight-arm salute, which is widely associated with fascist ideology.

Di Canio's action immediately sparked outrage and condemnation, both within the footballing community and among the public.

The fascist salute has deep historical connotations and is associated with totalitarian regimes and extremist ideologies.

Its use on a football field was seen as deeply offensive and inappropriate, given the sport's diverse and inclusive nature.

Di Canio's action led to a significant fallout for the player. He was fined by Lazio and received a suspension from the Italian Football Federation

(FIGC). Additionally, his reputation was tarnished, and he faced criticism from many quarters for the gesture. In the aftermath of the incident, Di Canio issued statements defending his actions, claiming that the gesture was not intended to promote any political ideology but was meant as a tribute to Lazio's fans. However, many viewed his explanation skeptically, and the incident left a lasting stain on his career.

Despite the controversy surrounding the "finger gesture," Paolo Di Canio remained a talented and mercurial footballer. His skill on the field was often overshadowed by the incident, but he continued to play at a high level for various clubs throughout his career.

While Di Canio's actions were regrettable and sparked widespread condemnation, the incident also raised important discussions about the responsibility of players as role models and the need for inclusivity and respect within football and society as a whole.

Chapter 9: Curiosities about the Rules of Football

9.1 *The Offside Rule: Gain insights into the nuances of the offside rule, one of the most debated and misunderstood aspects of football.*

The offside rule is a fundamental and integral part of football that has sparked countless debates, discussions, and controversies over the years.

It is designed to ensure fairness and maintain balance between attacking and defending teams, but its intricacies can be perplexing even to seasoned football fans.

The concept of the offside rule traces its roots back to the early days of football in the mid-19th century. In those early years, the offside rule was quite different from what we know today.

Initially, the rule stated that any player ahead of the ball was in an offside position, which led to frequent stoppages and limited attacking play.

As the game evolved, there was a need to strike a balance between promoting attacking football while preventing players from simply hanging around the opponent's goal.

In 1866, the first major change to the offside rule occurred, as the "three-player" system was introduced.

This rule stated that a player was only offside if they were ahead of the ball and the second-last defender when the ball was played to them.

This modification eased the burden on attacking players and encouraged a more fluid and dynamic style of play.

Over the years, several modifications were made to refine the offside rule further.

In 1925, the number of defenders required to be between the attacking player and the goal line was reduced to two, creating the offside rule that is more familiar to modern fans.

This change enhanced attacking opportunities and increased goal-scoring, leading to a more exciting and entertaining game.

To comprehend the offside rule, it is essential to understand the concept of being in an "offside position."

A player is considered to be in an offside position if they are nearer to their opponent's goal line than both the ball and the second-last defender when the ball is played to them.

However, it is crucial to note that being in an offside position is not an offense itself.

A player is only penalized for being offside if they are actively involved in the play.

This means that simply being in an offside position when a teammate passes the ball is not enough to warrant a foul.

A player is deemed to be actively involved in the play and committing an offside offense if they:

- Gain an advantage from being in an offside position: This can happen if the player receives the ball directly from a teammate or if the ball rebounds off an opponent.
- Interfere with an opponent: A player is considered to interfere with an opponent if they prevent the opponent from playing the ball or if they obstruct the opponent's line of vision or movement.
- Gain an advantage from being in an offside position: This can happen if the player receives the ball directly from a teammate or if the ball rebounds off an opponent.

Defensive teams often employ tactical strategies known as "offside traps" to catch attacking players in offside positions.

This involves the defenders stepping up in unison to catch the attacking player offside when the ball is played. If executed correctly, the offside trap can be an effective way to frustrate opposing attackers and disrupt their rhythm.

9.2 *The Golden Goal Rule: Learn about the brief experiment with the golden goal rule, where the first team to score in extra time would win the match.*

The Golden Goal rule was an experimental rule in football that aimed to add excitement and drama to extra time periods in knockout matches. It was introduced to encourage more attacking play during the extra time and to avoid the necessity of penalty shootouts to determine the winner.

Although it was implemented for only a short period, the Golden Goal rule left a lasting impact on football and sparked both praise and controversy among fans and pundits.

The concept of the Golden Goal rule was first introduced by the International Football Association Board (IFAB) in 1993. The rule aimed to address the issue of prolonged and often cautious extra time periods in knockout matches.

During regular extra time, teams would sometimes adopt defensive tactics to avoid conceding goals, leading to dull and uneventful play.

The IFAB believed that introducing a rule where the first team to score a goal during extra time would automatically win the match would encourage more attacking play and increase the chances of a decisive result before the match headed to penalties.

The Golden Goal rule made its first appearance at the European Championship (Euro) in 1996, held in England.

It was the first major international tournament to test the experimental rule.

The rule was applied in all knockout matches, starting from the quarterfinals.

The first-ever Golden Goal in an official tournament was scored by Czech Republic's Karel Poborský, who netted the decisive goal in the quarterfinal match against Portugal, securing the Czech Republic's place in the semifinals.

The Golden Goal rule created a sense of urgency and drama, with fans on the edge of their seats, anticipating a sudden and dramatic end to the match.

Matches became more thrilling and unpredictable, as any goal could prove to be the winner.

However, not everyone was in favor of the Golden Goal rule.

Critics argued that the rule put too much emphasis on luck and randomness.

A team could dominate the match for the majority of regular time, only to concede a single goal in extra time and lose the match without a chance to respond.

Additionally, the Golden Goal rule was seen as potentially unfair to teams that had worked hard to reach extra time, as it could lead to a sudden and unexpected exit from the tournament without having a proper opportunity to overturn the deficit.

Several memorable Golden Goal moments emerged during Euro 1996.

One of the most iconic moments was Oliver Bierhoff's Golden Goal for Germany in the final against the Czech Republic. Bierhoff's goal secured Germany's victory and made him the first player to score a Golden Goal in a major international final.

Another unforgettable moment was Paul Gascoigne's near miss during the same match.

Gascoigne came agonizingly close to scoring a Golden Goal for England in the semifinals against Germany, as his outstretched leg narrowly missed connecting with the ball in front of an open net.

Following the success and excitement generated by the Golden Goal rule at Euro 1996, FIFA decided to adopt the rule for the first time at the FIFA World Cup during the 1998 tournament held in France. The rule was implemented in all knockout matches, starting from the round of 16.

The Golden Goal rule made its World Cup debut in a dramatic round of 16 match between France and Paraguay.

The match went into extra time, and Laurent Blanc became the first player to score a Golden Goal in World Cup history, sending the host nation into the quarterfinals.

The Golden Goal rule had its swansong at the Euro 2004 in Portugal.

After nearly a decade of implementing the rule in major international tournaments, it was met with mixed reviews from players, coaches, and fans.

Some believed that it added excitement and tension to the matches, while others felt that it was too arbitrary and often led to conservative play during extra time.

In the Euro 2004 quarterfinal match between Greece and the Czech Republic, Traianos Dellas scored the final Golden Goal in the history of major international tournaments, propelling Greece to the semifinals.

Despite its moments of excitement and drama, the Golden Goal rule was eventually abolished by IFAB in 2004.

The decision came after much deliberation and feedback from various stakeholders in the football community.

Critics of the rule argued that it often led to defensive and cautious play during extra time, as teams were more concerned with avoiding conceding a goal than scoring one. Additionally, the arbitrary nature of the rule meant that a single moment of brilliance or a moment of misfortune could determine the outcome of a match.

As a result, IFAB decided to revert to the traditional format of extra time, where two periods of 15 minutes would be played, and if no winner was decided, the match would proceed to a penalty shootout.

9.3 *The Recent Rule Changes: Explore the recent rule changes implemented by football's governing bodies to enhance the fairness and flow of the game.*

Football, like any sport, is constantly evolving to adapt to the changing times and improve the overall experience for players, officials, and fans.

Over the years, football's governing bodies, including FIFA and IFAB (International Football Association Board), have introduced various rule changes aimed at improving the fairness, safety, and flow of the game.

Let's delves into some of the most significant recent rule changes that have shaped the modern football landscape.

- **VAR (Video Assistant Referee):**

One of the most revolutionary changes in recent football history is the introduction of Video Assistant Referee, commonly known as VAR.

Implemented in various top-flight leagues and major international tournaments, VAR uses video technology to assist on-field referees in making critical decisions.

Introduced to address contentious and game-changing moments, VAR allows match officials to review incidents such as potential goals, penalties, red cards, and mistaken identity. The VAR team watches multiple camera angles to provide the on-field referee with additional information, helping them make more accurate decisions.

While VAR has significantly reduced errors and improved decision-making, it has also been met with mixed reactions.

Critics argue that VAR can slow down the pace of the game and create uncertainty among players and fans, particularly during lengthy reviews.

Despite its controversies, VAR remains an essential tool in maintaining fairness and reducing mistakes in football.

- **Law Changes for Handball:**

In recent years, the interpretation of handball incidents has been a contentious issue in football. To provide greater clarity and consistency, IFAB introduced changes to the handball rule in 2019. The new law states that a player will be penalized for handball if they make their body "unnaturally bigger" by extending their arms beyond the body's silhouette.

The updated handball rule aims to differentiate between accidental and intentional handball offenses, thus reducing controversial decisions that were often subject to interpretation. However, the law has led to debates and frustrations among players, coaches, and fans, as the distinction between natural and unnatural handball remains a matter of debate.

- **Drop Ball Rule Modification:**

Another recent rule change involved the modification of the drop ball procedure. Traditionally, drop balls were used to restart play after a stoppage where the referee was required to make a decision.
However, in the modern game, the drop ball often resulted in contested situations and potential unfair advantages.
To address this issue, IFAB introduced a change in 2019, allowing the team that last touched the ball before play was stopped to regain possession.
This modification eliminated the competitive aspect of the drop ball and ensured a fairer restart.

- **Goalkeeper Movement During Penalties:**

To address concerns about goalkeepers gaining unfair advantages during penalty kicks, IFAB implemented a new rule in 2019.

The rule states that goalkeepers must have at least one foot on or in line with the goal line when the penalty is taken.

Previously, goalkeepers often gained an advantage by moving forward from the goal line before the penalty was struck, potentially making it harder for the penalty taker to score.

The new rule aims to level the playing field and ensure fairer penalty scenarios.

Chapter 10: The Attractiveness of Arab Leagues in Football

Football, being the world's most popular sport, has an incredible ability to transcend borders and unite people from different cultures and backgrounds.

In recent years, football in Arab countries has witnessed remarkable growth, with their leagues attracting significant attention both domestically and internationally.

The increasing popularity of Arab leagues can be attributed to several factors that have contributed to their rapid development and rising allure.

In this chapter, we explore the key elements behind the attractiveness of Arab leagues in football, shedding light on their emergence as prominent players in the global football landscape.

10.1 *Analysis of positive and negative aspects*

Pros of Playing in Arab Leagues:

- **High Wages and Lucrative Contracts:**

One of the primary attractions for football players to join Arab leagues is the promise of high wages and lucrative contracts. Clubs in the Middle East and Gulf region often possess significant financial resources, enabling them to offer substantial salaries to foreign players. The allure of earning substantial amounts of money during their careers entices many footballers to consider the option of playing in these leagues. For players looking to secure their financial future or support their families, the financial incentives offered by Arab clubs can be highly appealing.

- **Tax Benefits and Financial Incentives:**

Another advantage of playing in Arab leagues is the tax benefits and financial incentives that are often part of the package. Some countries in the region have more lenient tax regulations for foreign players, or they may even offer tax-free incomes. This can result

140

in players retaining a larger portion of their earnings, which further adds to the financial appeal of joining these leagues. Moreover, some clubs may offer additional perks, such as housing allowances, transportation, and other bonuses, making the overall compensation package quite enticing.

- **Modern Infrastructure and Quality of Life:**

Arab countries have witnessed significant economic growth and development in recent decades, leading to modern infrastructure and a high standard of living. Football players who relocate to these countries can expect to find state-of-the-art stadiums, training facilities, and top-notch medical support. Additionally, the quality of life outside the football field is generally comfortable, with access to modern amenities, entertainment, and recreational opportunities. For players seeking a comfortable and modern lifestyle, Arab leagues can provide an excellent environment.

Cons of Playing in Arab Leagues:

- **Cultural and Language Barriers:**

One of the primary challenges for football players moving to Arab leagues is the significant cultural and language barriers they may encounter.

Arab countries have their own unique customs, traditions, and ways of life, which can be vastly different from what players are accustomed to in their home countries.

Adjusting to a new culture can be daunting and may lead to feelings of isolation and homesickness. Moreover, the language barrier can pose communication difficulties both on and off the field, potentially affecting team dynamics and player-coach relationships.

Arab countries often have strong religious traditions, and players from different cultural backgrounds may need to adapt to different religious practices and observances.

For example, during the holy month of Ramadan, Muslim players may fast from sunrise to sunset, affecting training schedules and match preparation. Non-Muslim players may need to be respectful and understanding of these practices.

- **Competitive Standards and Development Opportunities:**

While Arab leagues have been growing in stature, some players may view them as less competitive compared to the top European leagues.

Playing in a league with lower competitive standards could hinder a player's development and limit opportunities to showcase their skills on a global stage.

The lack of exposure to top-level competition and scouting networks may impact their chances of representing their national teams or attracting interest from bigger clubs in Europe.

- **Limited Global Visibility and Marketability:**

Arab leagues, despite their growth, may still have limited global visibility compared to the major European leagues like the English Premier League or La Liga.

This reduced exposure can impact a player's marketability and endorsement opportunities. Players seeking to build a brand and secure endorsement deals may find it more challenging to do so in leagues with less international recognition.

- **Distance from Family and Support Systems:**

Playing in Arab leagues often involves significant geographical distance from a player's home and support systems, such as family, friends, and cultural familiarity.

The isolation from loved ones and the comfort of familiar surroundings can lead to feelings of loneliness and homesickness.

Maintaining strong family ties and coping with life's challenges without immediate familial support may pose emotional and psychological challenges for players.

- **Adverse Weather Conditions:**

The extreme climate in Arab countries, particularly during the summer months, can be a significant drawback for some players.

The scorching heat and high humidity levels can take a toll on players' physical performance and increase the risk of heat-related illnesses.

Training and playing in such conditions require additional precautions and careful management to ensure player safety and well-being.

Despite these challenges, some players may still choose to play in Arab leagues because of the financial incentives, cultural experiences, and potential for personal growth.

However, it is essential for players to weigh these cons carefully against their career aspirations and personal preferences.

10.2 *Financial Investments: Elevating Arab Leagues to New Heights in Football*

In the dynamic and competitive world of football, financial investments play a pivotal role in shaping the success and growth of leagues and clubs. Arab countries, endowed with vast reserves of oil and gas, have harnessed their economic strength to channel substantial financial resources into the development of football. These investments have transformed Arab leagues, propelling them to the forefront of the global football landscape and garnering attention from players, fans, and media worldwide. In this section, we delve into the significance and impact of financial investments in Arab leagues, as well as explore examples of clubs that epitomize the wealth-driven transformation of football in the region.

The immense wealth of several Arab countries has created an opportunity to invest significantly in football infrastructure, talent acquisition, youth development, and marketing.

The vision to elevate the status of Arab leagues and clubs on the international stage has been achieved through strategic and substantial financial backing. The key areas where financial investments have led to notable improvements in Arab football are as follows:

• Modern Stadiums and Facilities:

With a commitment to building state-of-the-art stadiums, Arab countries have transformed the football landscape in the region.

These modern venues not only cater to the needs of players and fans but also align with international standards for hosting major football events.

From iconic architectural designs to innovative technologies, Arab stadiums have become symbols of progress and ambition in the world of football.

• High-Profile Player Acquisitions:

Financial prowess has enabled Arab clubs to compete in the global transfer market for high-profile players. By attracting renowned football stars from Europe, South America, and other regions, Arab leagues have elevated their competitive level and gained international recognition.

These marquee signings not only enhance the quality of football played but also generate excitement and media attention, boosting the leagues' popularity.

• Youth Development Programs:

Investments in football extend beyond the elite level to grassroots and youth development.

Arab countries have established comprehensive youth academies and programs to nurture local talent from a young age.

The objective is not only to produce skilled players for local clubs but also to contribute to national team success.

By investing in youth development, Arab leagues are ensuring sustainable growth and continuity in their football prowess.

- **Marketing and Global Branding:**

Financial investments have also been directed toward marketing and branding of Arab leagues and clubs. Robust marketing campaigns, sponsorship deals, and media partnerships have increased the global visibility of Arab football.

As a result, these leagues have become attractive destinations for international fans and investors, further expanding their reach beyond the region.

10.3 *Acquisition of Foreign Talents: Enriching Arab Leagues with Global Flair*

In the ever-evolving world of football, the quest for excellence and success knows no boundaries.

Arab leagues have embraced this ethos by actively pursuing foreign talents to bolster the technical quality and competitiveness of their football competitions.

The acquisition of international stars from diverse footballing backgrounds has not only elevated the standard of play in Arab leagues but has also enriched the game with global flair and diversity.

In this section, we delve into the significance and impact of the acquisition of foreign talents in Arab leagues, exploring the reasons behind this trend and providing a comprehensive list of notable players who have chosen to ply their trade in the region.

I report to you below a list of players who until 2020 moved to the Arab leagues:

Player	Nationality	Team	Year of transfer
Omar Abdulrahman	UAE	Al Ain FC	2010
Asamoah Gyan	Ghana	Al Ain FC	2011
Grafite	Brazil	Al Ahli Dubai	2011
Ricardo Oliveira	Brazil	Al Jazira Club	2012
Jo	Brazil	Al Shabab	2014
Ignacio Scocco	Argentina	Al Ain FC	2012
Bafétimbi Gomis	France	Al Hilal	2018
Emmanuel Adebayor	Togo	Al Ittihad	2011
Andre-Pierre Gignac	France	Umm Salal SC	2013
Carlos Eduardo	Brazil	Al Hilal	2015
Sadio Diallo	Guinea	Al Raed	2019
Jorge Valdivia	Chile	Al Ittihad	2018
Mark Bresciano	Australia	Al Nasr FC	2012
Joel Obi	Nigeria	Al Arabi	2018
Youssef El-Arabi	Morocco	Al Duhail SC	2019
Mauro Zarate	Argentina	Al Nassr	2017
Leandro Damiao	Brazil	Al Wahda	2019
Wilfried Bony	Ivory Coast	Al Arabi	2020
Romarinho	Brazil	Al Ittihad FC	2018
Emmanuel Emenike	Nigeria	Al Ain	2017
Ismael Bangoura	Guinea	Al Raed	2019
Diego Cavalieri	Brazil	Al Nassr	2018

10.4 _The boom of the Arab transfer market 2022-2023_

Player	From	To	Annual salary
Cristiano Ronaldo	Manchester Un.	Al Nassr	200 millions
Karim Benzema	Real Madrid	Al Ittihad	100 millions
Neymar	PSG	Al Hilal	80 millions
Riyad Mahrez	Manchester City	Al-Ahli	30 millions
Kalidou Koulibaly	Chelsea	Al Hilal	30 millions
N'golo Kantè	Chelsea	Al Ittihad	25 millions
Ruben Neves	Wolverhampton	Al Hilal	25 millions
Sadio Manè	Bayern München	Al Nassr	25 millions
Marcelo Brozovic	FC Internazionale	Al Nassr	20 millions
Roberto Firmino	Liverpool	Al-Ahli	20 millions
Sergej Milinkovic-Savic	Lazio	Al Hilal	20 millions
Edouard Mendy	Chelsea	Al-Ahli	12 millions
Jordan Henderson	Liverpool	Al Ettifaq	10 millions

In the latest 2023/2024 transfer window, negotiations have literally gone wild.

We witnessed a true migratory phenomenon of some crystal-clear talents playing in the top global leagues and the most prestigious teams in the world.

Among the footballers who have succumbed to the advances of the Saudi league, we also have winners of international trophies and some of the strongest players of all time like Karim Benzema and Cristiano

Ronaldo.

This transfer window has all the right ingredients to mark a new chapter in the history of international football.
The world is changing, evolving, and even the world of football, and then let's be honest...
...wouldn't you go to Arabia to do what you do but get paid 10 times more?

No matter what.

Even though the football world is constantly changing, and the balance is shifting towards the Saudi League, no pharaonic contract will be able to buy and change our passion for this sport.

Football,

                Soccer,

Fútbol,

                Fußball,

Calcio,

                Futebol,

Voetbal,

                Fotboll,

Zúqiú,

                Sakka,

Kurat Alqadam,

                Kaduregel,

Phutabal,

                Mpira wa miguu,

Bóng dá,

                Pilka nozna,

Labdarúgás, Fotbal

                Chukgu…

…call it as you want

but please, **don't stop loving this game.**

153

Thank you for getting here.

If thanks to this book you have discovered things you didn't know and increased your football baggage, I ask you for help with a short review.

And remember...

...*don't stop loving this game.*

Declan R. Kensington